CIVILIAN-BASED DEFENSE

CIVILIAN-BASED DEFENSE

A POST-MILITARY WEAPONS SYSTEM

Gene Sharp

With the assistance of Bruce Jenkins

PRINCETON UNIVERSITY PRESS   PRINCETON NEW JERSEY

Copyright © 1990 by Princeton University Press
Published by Princeton University Press, 41 William Street,
Princeton, New Jersey 08540
In the United Kingdom: Princeton University Press, Oxford
All Rights Reserved

Library of Congress Cataloging-in-Publication Data
Sharp, Gene.
Civilian-based defense : a post-military weapons system /
by Gene Sharp ; with the assistance of Bruce Jenkins
p. cm.
ISBN 0-691-07809-2 (alk. paper)
1. Civilian-based defense.   I. Jenkins, Bruce.   II. Title.
UA10.7.S47   1990
363.3'5—dc20   90-8222   CIP

This book has been composed in Adobe Laser Palatino

Princeton University Press books are printed
on acid-free paper, and meet the guidelines
for permanence and durability of the Committee
on Production Guidelines for Book Longevity
of the Council on Library Resources

Printed in the United States of America by
Princeton University Press, Princeton, New Jersey

10 9 8 7 6 5 4 3 2 1

Contents

Preface

CIVILIAN-BASED DEFENSE is intended to be a substantive introduction to the developing policy of civilian-based defense. Instead of military weaponry, civilian-based defense applies the power of society itself to deter and defend against internal usurpations and foreign invaders. The weapons are psychological, social, economic, and political. They are wielded by the general population and the institutions of the society.

The propositions of this book are two: that civilian-based defense policies against internal takeovers and foreign aggression can be developed, and that dictatorships and oppression can be prevented and disintegrated by the capacity to wage powerful nonviolent struggle. Massive noncooperation and defiance would aim to prevent attackers from establishing effective control over the defending society, to deny the attackers their objectives, and to subvert the reliability of the attackers' administrators and military forces.

Civilian-based defense is presented for research, investigation, and public and governmental evaluation. In some countries limited aspects of the policy have already been incorporated into existing defense policies.

My objective has been in part to prepare a book that stimulates thought among members of the general public who are searching for better answers to our defense problems. The aim has also been to present new information, conceptions, and options that merit attention by defense analysts, security specialists, government officials, military officers, strategists of nonviolent struggle, scholars, students, and members of society's voluntary organizations who would play indispensible roles in civilian-based defense.

This volume is focused on the broad security problems that may be faced by many countries, not only those of a single part of the world, in contrast to my earlier book *Making Europe Unconquerable*. Given a desire for democracy and independence, therefore, this presentation of civilian-based defense is of interest to very diverse countries. All countries, no matter what their political or economic status, must concern themselves with the possibility of foreign invasion or internal usurpation. These are the problems addressed in this book. Using this broad presentation, the people of virtually all countries will be able to assess the possible relevance of civilian-based defense for their particular societies, each with its own traditions, security threats, and military options.

This book was originally suggested by Sanford Thatcher of Princeton University Press some years ago. His encouragement, perceptive recommendations, critical comments, support, and patience have enabled the project finally to come to fruition. Since Mr. Thatcher's departure from the Press, Ms. Gail Ullman, as Social Science Editor, has ably seen the manuscript through the final stages. Charles Ault at the Press made superb editorial recommendations.

For the past year I have been extremely fortunate at the Albert Einstein Institution to have had the most able assistance of Bruce Jenkins in the preparation of this book. His research, perceptive substantive criticisms and suggestions, as well as his editorial skills, have made this a far better book than it would otherwise have been.

I am grateful to the Albert Einstein Institution and to its donors and staff for making this work possible. With expanded support for such organizations, many other studies of the nature and potential of nonviolent struggle as a substitute for violence against aggression, dictatorships, genocide, and oppression will become possible.

During the 1980s we witnessed the most important worldwide expansion of the practical use of nonviolent struggle that has ever occurred. From Tallinn to Nablus, Rangoon to Santiago, Pretoria to Prague, Beijing to Berlin, people around the world are ever more employing nonviolent struggle to assert their rights for freedom, independence, and justice. Scholarly investigations, hard-headed assessments, and sophisticated strategic analyses are now needed to understand this technique further and to increase its effectiveness. This book is only one of many that need to be written on the nature, problems, and potential of nonviolent struggle. These will help us to assess what roles nonviolent struggle and civilian-based defense may play in confronting, and solving, the problems of dictatorship, genocide, oppression, and war.

Gene Sharp

Albert Einstein Institution
1430 Massachuetts Avenue
Cambridge, Massachusetts 02138

10 January 1990

CIVILIAN-BASED DEFENSE

One

Defense without War?

The Need for Defense

Two Things are certain about the future of politics and international relations: conflict is inevitable and effective defense will be required against internal usurpers and international aggressors.

All political societies whose members do not wish to become victims of these attacks need—among other things—a security policy and a weapons system of some type to struggle against them. This policy and weapons system must be able to accomplish two tasks: to deter and to defend.

First, the weapons system needs to be sufficiently strong and well enough prepared to have a high probability of deterring internal usurpation and international aggression. The aim of *deterrence* is to convince potential attackers not to attack because the consequences could be unacceptably costly to them, including the failure to gain their objectives. Deterrence is a crucial part of the much broader process of *dissuasion*: to induce potential attackers to abandon their intent to attack as the result of any of several influences, including rational argument, moral appeal, distraction, and nonprovocative policies, as well as deterrence.

However, a major problem exists. Dissuasion may fail, and no deterrent can ever be guaranteed to deter. Consequently, the results of the failure of deterrence and the use of one's chosen weaponry must be survivable and remediable.

Second, if and when deterrence fails the weapons system must be able to defend effectively. Defense should be understood literally as protection, preservation, and the warding off of danger. The means used to defend must be capable of neutralizing and ending the attack but must not destroy the society being defended. The defense capacity must be able to cause the attackers to desist and withdraw, or to defeat them, and to restore the society's prior condition of peace, autonomy, and chosen constitutional system.

Most people and governments have believed that only military means can deter foreign aggression and defend against it. Opinions differ on the adequacy of military policies to accomplish those tasks and on the severity of the problems they entail. These opinions include the view, on the one extreme, that strong military means constitute the only realistic option in face of international dangers, and that to weaken—even worse, to eliminate—those means is both politically and morally irresponsible. On the other extreme is the pacifist view that war itself is worse than any other political evil and that individuals and whole societies ought therefore to oppose, and refuse to participate in, all military action and preparations. There are many other views and combinations of opinions between these two extremes.

This book is not about any of those views, and an assessment of the merits and relevance of the analysis here does not depend on one's opinions about the relative adequacy of military policies or one's convictions concerning the acceptability of "just wars" or of "pacifism." Indeed, both of those extreme positions may today be inadequate or incomplete on both political and moral grounds. The important point here is that today virtually no one claims that military means are perfect or denies that military means are associated with very serious problems and dangers. In addition, virtually no one would argue that military means always succeed in gaining their objectives. Massive devastation aside, defeat is always possible.

The extreme destructiveness of modern military technology has stimulated a great variety of reactions and proposed alternatives. Few of these attempt both to prevent or limit attacks and destruction *and* to provide a defense as we have defined it.

One response has been to call for the restructuring of military forces along strictly defensive lines. Alternately called "defensive defense," "nonoffensive defense," and "nonprovocative defense," this approach has been well developed in Western Europe and bears important similarities with the long-standing defense policy of Switzerland. In the Swiss policy both weaponry and strategic planning are designed for exclusively defensive use, without preparations or the capacity to counterattack the territory of possible aggressors.

The exponents of this approach—which has several variants—have proposed military forces outfitted with less destructive weapons that have limited mobility and range, making them unsuited for offensive purposes. For example, anti-tank weapons are favored over tanks themselves, and short-range fighter planes are preferred to long-range bombers or rockets. Some exponents have also proposed adoption of strictly defensive strategies for using that equipment, without contingency plans and preparations for offensive attacks, or even counterattacks. Such defensively structured forces, it is argued, would reduce the threat perception of other countries, making preemptive attacks more unlikely. In some countries, as in West Germany, these ideas have gained a certain credibility. They merit serious critical examination as a proposed policy to assist deterrence and defense without weapons of mass destruction.

A detailed criticism of "defensive defense" is not possible here, but it is necessary to note that this approach clearly contains some serious problems. First, the danger of escalation of a war would remain a possibility. On the aggressors' side, if the limited military defensive measures proved to be a serious impediment to successful aggression, the attackers would likely increase the severity and destructiveness of their onslaught. On the defenders' side, if their limited defensive military measures were not deemed to be adequate, there would be pressure, if the capacity existed (or could be quickly developed or procured) to use more destructive weapons.

Second, "defensive defense" measures would almost guarantee vast casualties among the civilian population. A military conflict without a traditional front and with numerous small military units widely dispersed throughout the territory is an invitation to high casualties. (The proposal to reduce this danger by declaring urban areas "open cities," which would not be defended militarily, does not eliminate this problem.) In certain respects, the "defensive defense" approach is basically a modification of guerrilla warfare for defense, generally combined with high technology military weapons for precision attacks on the invaders. The basic problems inherent in guerrilla warfare for defense apply to "defensive defense." That policy, when applied, is likely therefore to have important similarities with the experience of guerrilla struggles in various countries, including Yugoslavia, occupied parts of the Soviet Union, Algeria, and Vietnam. In such cases, the number of dead among the defending population was exceptionally high, often more than ten percent of the whole population. Vast physical and social destruction was also typical. In densely populated Central Europe, where "defensive defense" proposals are to be applied, the level of casualties and destruction could be catastrophic. Finally, even in the case of victory, there are likely to be long-term social, economic, political, and psychological consequences due to the conflict itself, including harm to the society's institutions and the buildup of military systems.

Military-based "defensive defense" therefore does not seem to be a satisfactory solution to our common dilemma of the need for deterrence and defense on the one hand and the massive destructiveness of present military technology on the other. Whatever may be our various opinions about military means in general, it is highly desirable to explore whatever nonmilitary alternatives may exist or could be developed to meet the needs of societies to deter and defend against external attacks and internal usurpations.

We do have some limited resources in the search for such nonmilitary alternative means of deterrence and defense. Large-scale noncooperation and defiance have already, in a number of cases, been improvised for defense against foreign aggression and internal usurpations. These cases are not usually well known, and their potential significance for defense has rarely been examined seriously. Yet they exist, thereby establishing that an alternative to military and paramilitary means for national defense is possible under at least certain circumstances. The important question, therefore, becomes how the potential of nonmilitary struggle can be developed so that its capacity in diverse cases will really deter attacks and, if need be, defend successfully against them. Can there be an effective post-military defense policy capable of providing deterrence and defense while avoiding the dangers of modern war?

Civilian-based Defense

This type of alternative policy is called *civilian-based defense* in the United States and usually *civilian defense* or *social defense* in Europe. The term indicates defense by civilians (as distinct from military personnel) using civilian means of struggle (as distinct from military and paramilitary means). This is a policy intended to deter and defeat foreign military invasions, occupations, and internal usurpations. The latter includes both executive usurpations and the more usual coups d'état, that is, seizures of the physical and political control of the state machinery, often by an elite political, military, or paramilitary group from within or without the established government. Such coups may be conducted purely internally or may receive foreign instigation and aid.

Deterrence and defense against external aggression and internal usurpation are to be accomplished by reliance on social, economic, political, and psychological weapons. (By "weapons" we mean those tools or means, not necessarily material, that may be used in fighting, whether in military or nonviolent conflicts.) In civilian-based defense these nonviolent weapons are used to wage widespread noncooperation and to offer massive public defiance. The aim is both to deny the attackers their objectives and to make impossible the consolidation of their rule, whether in the form of foreign administration, a puppet regime, or a government of usurpers. This noncooperation and defiance is also combined with other forms of action intended to subvert the loyalty of the attackers' troops and functionaries, to promote their unreliability in carrying out orders and repression, and even to induce them to mutiny.

Civilian-based defense is an application, in a refined and developed form, of the general technique of nonviolent action, or nonviolent struggle, to the problems of national defense. It is to be applied by the general population, by specific groups most affected by the attackers' objectives and action, and by the society's institutions. Which of these are most involved varies with the attackers' aims—whether they are economic, ideological, political, or another sort.

Civilian-based defense is meant to be waged by the population and its institutions on the basis of advance preparation, planning, and training. These in turn would be based upon the findings of basic research into nonviolent resistance, upon in-depth analysis of the political system of the attackers, and upon intensive problem-solving research, such as how to increase the population's capacity to continue resistance in the face of severe repression or how best to maintain effective channels of communication when under attack. Understanding of the requirements to make these nonviolent forms of struggle as effective as possible and insights into the ways to aggravate the attackers' weaknesses are the foundations for developing successful strategies of civilian-based defense.

Civilian-based defense rests on the theory that political power, whether of domestic or foreign origin, is derived from sources *within* each society. By denying or severing these sources of power, populations can control rulers and defeat foreign aggressors. This theory will be examined more closely in Chapter Two. In Chapter Three, we will examine the application of this theory of "dependent rulers" through the broader technique of nonviolent action, from which civilian-based defense derives numerous precepts. Chapter Four will then sketch the outlines of a possible civilian-based defense policy. This policy, as with most defense measures, is meant to be waged on the basis of advance preparation, planning, and training. Chapter Five will examine several of the steps that can be taken (or, as in several cases, have *already* been taken) in investigating, preparing, and implementing a policy of civilian-based defense.

Historical Prototypes

We have major resources in earlier improvised struggles from which we can learn in preparing for future civilian-based defense against aggressors. We can learn about the nature of nonviolent struggle and its potential by examining cases involving a great variety of issues.

As the following examples reveal, the heritage of nonviolent struggle is quite diverse and extends far beyond struggles for national defense purposes. Nonviolent action has played a major role in resistance against dictatorships, in struggles for achieving greater freedom, in campaigns against social oppression, in opposition to unwanted political changes, and in struggles against colonial rule and for national independence. Contrary to usual perceptions, these means of struggle—by protest, noncooperation, and disruptive intervention—have played major historical roles in all parts of the world. These experiences include cases in which historical attention has been primarily focused on the violence that occurred simultaneously or later on in the conflict.

Relevant resistance movements and revolutions against internal oppression and dictatorships in recent decades are the Polish movements of 1956, 1970–1971, and 1976; the Polish workers' movement, 1980 to 1989, for an independent trade union and political democratization; the 1944 nonviolent revolutions in El Salvador and Guatemala against established military dictatorships; the civil rights struggles in the United States in the 1950s and 1960s; the 1978–1979 revolution against the Shah in Iran; the 1953 East German Rising; major aspects of the 1956–1957 Hungarian revolution; the 1963 Buddhist campaign against the Ngo Dinh Diem government in South Vietnam and the 1966 Buddhist campaign against the Saigon regime; the 1953 strike movement at Vorkuta and other prison camps in the Soviet Union; and civil rights and Jewish activist struggles in the USSR in the 1970s and 1980s.

Earlier instances of politically significant nonviolent struggle against domestic tyranny and foreign rule include the American colonial nonviolent revolution (1765–1775), which produced major victories for the Americans and replaced most British governments in the North American colonies; Hungarian passive resistance against Austrian rule, especially 1850–1867; Finland's disobedience and political noncooperation against Russia, 1898–1905; major aspects of the Russian Revolution of 1905, and the February Revolution of 1917 (before the October Bolshevik coup d'état); the Korean nonviolent protest (which failed) against Japanese rule, 1919–1922; and several Gandhi-led Indian independence campaigns, especially in 1930–1931.

Other countries in which significant nonviolent struggles have occurred in the 1970s and 1980s include Chile, Iran, Brazil, Mexico, China, the Soviet Union, Haiti, the Philippines, India, South Africa, Burma, Hungary, South Korea, New Caledonia, Czechoslovakia, Pakistan, Panama, and the Israeli-occupied Palestinian territories.

To the surprise of many people, nonviolent struggle during 1989 became a major characteristic of the Chinese pro-democracy movement. The first phase of that struggle ended with the massacre in Tiananmen Square and elsewhere in Beijing, but the struggle then gradually entered another phase. The Soviet Union during 1989 experienced extremely widespread and massive nonviolent struggles by, among others, coal miners, factory workers, and various nationalities (especially the Estonians, Latvians, Lithuanians, Armenians, and Georgians, some of whom demanded secession from the Soviet Union). Later in 1989, nonviolent revolutions shook East Germany, Czechoslovakia, and Bulgaria with amazing rapidity. It is impossible to predict where the next cases will occur.

Most people are unaware that, in addition to the above types of cases, unrefined nonviolent forms of struggle have also been used as a major means of defense against foreign invaders or internal usurpers.

In this chapter we shall sketch four cases of improvised nonviolent struggle for national defense, two against internal coups d'état and two against foreign military invasions and occupations. The anti-coup cases are the resistance to the Kapp Putsch in Weimar Germany in 1920 and the opposition to the attempt by French military officers in Algeria to overthrow the government of President Charles de Gaulle in 1961. The anti-aggression cases are the German attempt to defend the Ruhr from the Franco-Belgian invasion and occupation in 1923 and the national defense struggle in Czechoslovakia against the Soviet and Warsaw Pact invasion and occupation in 1968–1969.

These cases are chosen because they are the clearest applications of nonviolent struggle for constitutional defense and national defense as far as we are now aware and because a reasonable amount of historical material is available on them. In all four cases, however, the resistance was improvised, and the populace, its institutions, and government apparently lacked any preparation, organization, training, appropriate equipment, and contingency planning in nonviolent resistance (all of which military-based defense usually enjoys). This lack is a grave weakness in these cases. One can imagine how successful wars would be if there were no prior organized armies, no training of soldiers, no development and amassing of weapons and ammunition, no studies of military strategy, no preparation of officers' corps, no arrangements for transportation and communication, and no emergency supplies of blood and provision for medical services. The four cases outlined below occurred under such conditions.

There have been other examples of improvised nonviolent struggle for national defense. These include major aspects of the Dutch anti-Nazi resistance, 1940–1945; major aspects of the Danish resistance to the German occupation, 1940–1945 (including the 1944 Copenhagen general strike); the largest parts of the Norwegian resistance to the Quisling regime; and governmental and popular resistance to nullify anti-Jewish measures in several Nazi-allied and Nazi-occupied countries, such as Bulgaria, Italy, France, and Denmark.

All these cases of improvised defense merit careful research, study, and analysis. Not all succeeded. (Nor have all prepared military defense struggles been successful, especially not in gaining their objectives.) These cases demonstrate—simply because they have occurred—that this type of defense struggle is possible. Their results show that nonviolent struggle for defense can be powerful and effective. The cases also provide important insights into the dynamics and problems of such conflicts.

Improvised Struggles against Coups d'État

The two cases of civilian struggle against coups d'état described here are very different. However, both demonstrate that the legitimate government may be saved by action of ordinary people, civil servants, or regular soldiers, acting nonviolently. The German and the French cases are not the only examples, however.

It is interesting that Lenin for several years after his coup in October 1917 was confronted by noncooperation from the old bureaucracy. Government employees caused very serious problems for the new Communist government after the Bolshevik seizure of the state apparatus from the provisional government and the various rival revolutionary parties. The problems were still severe more than four years later. In March 1922, Lenin declared at the Eleventh Congress of the Russian Communist Party that "the political lesson" of 1921 had been that control of the seats of power does not necessarily mean control of the bureaucracy. He stated that the Communists "scatter orders right and left, but the result is quite different from what they want."

Other cases meriting research and analysis include the general strike in Haiti against temporary President Pierre-Louis in 1957, the successful noncooperation against a military coup in Bolivia in 1978, and Polish popular noncooperation against the regime of General Jaruzelski following the coup in 1981 (although the resistance was not widespread in the bureaucracy, police, or military forces).

Germany, 1920

In 1920, Germany's new Weimar Republic, already facing very severe economic and political problems, was attacked by a coup d'état organized by Dr. Wolfgang Kapp and Lieutenant-General Walter von Lüttwitz, with the backing of General Erich Ludendorff, who had in 1917 been virtual dictator of Germany. While most of the German army remained "neutral"—neither participating in nor opposing the coup—ex-soldiers and civilians organized in *Freikorps* units occupied Berlin on March 12. The legal democratic government under President Friedrich Ebert fled, eventually to Stuttgart.

While the Kappists in Berlin declared a new government, the legal government in flight proclaimed that it was the duty of all citizens to obey only it. The *Länder* (states) were directed to refuse all cooperation with those who had attacked the Republic.

After a strike of workers against the coup broke out in Berlin, the Social Democratic Party issued a proclamation calling for a general strike, under the names of President Ebert and other Social Democratic ministers (but without their official approval). The Kappists were quickly confronted with large-scale noncooperation. Civil servants and conservative government bureaucrats refused to cooperate with the usurpers. Qualified men refused to accept posts in the upstart regime. All along the line people denied authority to the usurpers and refused to assist them. On March 15, the legal government refused to compromise with the usurpers, and the Kappists' power further disintegrated. Many leaflets calling for resistance, entitled "The Collapse of the Military Dictatorship," were showered on the capital by airplane. Repression was often harsh. Some strikers were shot to death.

However, the impact of noncooperation grew. On March 17, the Berlin Security Police demanded Kapp's resignation. The same day, Kapp resigned and fled to Sweden. That night, many of his aides left Berlin in civilian clothes, and General von Lüttwitz resigned. Some bloody clashes had occurred in the midst of the predominantly nonviolent noncooperation. The *Freikorps* units then resumed obedience to the legal government and marched out of Berlin. As they did so, however, they killed and wounded some unsympathetic civilians. The coup was defeated by the combined action of workers, civil servants, bureaucrats, and the general population, who collectively refused the popular and administrative cooperation that the usurpers required to make their claims to power effective.

Other grave internal problems continued for the Weimar Republic. However, it had withstood its first frontal attack by the use of popular and governmental noncooperation and defiance against its internal attackers.

France, 1961

Early in April 1961, French President Charles de Gaulle indicated that he was abandoning the attempt to keep Algeria French. Then, in

French-ruled Algeria on the night of April 21–22, the French First Foreign Legion Parachute Regiment rebelled and captured control of the
city of Algiers from the legitimate French officials, while other rebel
military units seized key points nearby. There was no serious opposition. At least three French generals in Algeria loyal to the legal government—including the Commander-in-Chief—were arrested by the rebels. This was the culmination of earlier policy conflicts between the
French army in Algeria and the civilian French government in Paris.

On April 22, the rebel "Military Command" declared a state of siege
in Algeria, announced it was taking over all powers of civil government, and would break any resistance. Four colonels had organized the
conspiracy, but this statement was issued under the names of four recently retired generals (Challe, Jouhaud, Zeller, and Salan). The next
day the coup was backed by General Nicot (acting head of the French
Air Staff), General Bigot (commanding the air force in Algiers), and
three other generals. The usurpers seized control of newspapers and
radio, giving them (they thought) a monopoly on communications in
French Algeria.

The French government in Paris was in trouble. Half a million French
troops were in Algeria, leaving very few operational units in France
itself. Two French divisions stationed in Germany were of doubtful
reliability. The loyalty of the paramilitary *Gendarmerie Nationale* and the
Compagnies Républicaines de Sécurité was also in doubt. It was feared
that a parallel coup might be attempted against the government in
Paris or that the air force might transport rebel troops to invade France
and oust the de Gaulle government. The success of the coup in Algiers
hinged on replacing the legal government in Paris.

On Sunday, April 23, the political parties and trade unions in France
held mass meetings, calling for a one-hour symbolic general strike the
next day to demonstrate that they would oppose the coup. That night,
de Gaulle broadcast a speech to the French nation, urging people to
defy and disobey the rebels: "In the name of France, I order that all
means—I repeat all means—be employed to bar the way everywhere
to these men until they are brought down. I forbid every Frenchman,
and in the first place every soldier, to carry out any of their orders."

The same night, Prime Minister Debré in his own broadcast warned
of preparations for an airborne attack and closed down the Paris airports. While stressing "all means"—which obviously included military
action—Debré placed his confidence in nonviolent means as he called
for popular action to persuade soldiers who might be flying in to resume loyalty to the legal government: "As soon as the sirens sound, go
there [to the airports] by foot or by car, to convince the mistaken soldiers of their huge error."

De Gaulle's broadcast from France was heard in Algeria via transistor radios by the population and members of the military forces, many of them conscript soldiers. Copies of the address were then duplicated and widely distributed. De Gaulle credited his talk with inducing widespread noncooperation and disobedience: "From then on, the revolt met with a passive resistance on the spot which became hourly more explicit."

On April 24, at 5:00 P.M., ten million workers took part in the symbolic general strike. De Gaulle invoked emergency powers accorded to the President by the constitution. Many right-wing sympathizers were arrested. At airfields, people prepared vehicles to be placed on runways to block their use if planes attempted to land. Guards were stationed at public buildings. A financial and shipping blockade was imposed on Algeria. That night General Crépin announced that French forces in Germany were loyal to the government, and the next morning they were ordered to Paris.

French troops in Algeria acted to support the de Gaulle government and to undermine the rebels. By Tuesday two-thirds of the available transport planes and many fighter planes had been flown out of Algeria, making them unavailable for an invasion of France. Other pilots pretended mechanical failures or blocked airfields. Army soldiers simply stayed in their barracks. There were many cases of deliberate inefficiency: orders from rebel officers were lost, files disappeared, there were delays in communications and transportation. The conscripts generally recognized the power of their noncooperation in support of the legal government. Leaders of the coup had to use many of their available forces to attempt to keep control and maintain order among the French troops in Algeria itself. Many officers temporarily avoided taking sides, waiting to see how the contest would go, preparing to join the winning side.

French civilians in Algeria, including the Algiers police, at first supported the coup. But civil servants and local government officials in the city of Algiers often resisted, hiding documents and personally withdrawing so as not to be seen as supporting the coup. On Tuesday evening, April 25, the Algiers police resumed support for the de Gaulle government. Internal disagreements developed among the leaders of the revolt, with some advocating violent measures. That night, in another broadcast, de Gaulle ordered loyal troops to fire at the rebels. There was no need, however. The coup had already been fatally undermined.

The leaders resolved to call off the attempted coup. The night of April 25–26, the First Foreign Legion Parachute Regiment withdrew from Algiers and rebels abandoned government buildings. General

Challe surrendered and the other three retired generals heading the revolt hid.

There were a few casualties, probably three killed and several wounded in Algeria and Paris. The attack had been decisively defeated by defiance and dissolution. De Gaulle remained President and Algeria became independent in 1962.

Improvised Struggles against Invasions

A very large number of cases exist of nonviolent struggle waged against foreign occupation—regimes that were established years, decades, or even centuries earlier. These cases include, for example, much of Irish resistance to English rule, the Hungarian resistance to Austrian rule, 1850–1867, and the Indian campaigns against British occupation in the first half of the twentieth century. The following cases are, however, more obviously relevant to our discussion. First, the resistance began virtually immediately at the time of the invasion and continued into the occupation. Second, both cases had official sponsorship from the government and major institutions of the society. They are, therefore, more appropriate as prototypes of what could be developed.

Germany, 1923

Probably the first case in history of nonviolent resistance as official government policy against a foreign invasion was the German struggle in the Ruhr against the French and Belgian occupation in 1923.

The Ruhr struggle is especially complex and covers the period from January 11 to September 26, 1923. It is impossible here to do more than mention some of its features. The French and Belgian invasion was launched to secure scheduled payments of reparations (following the First World War) despite Germany's extreme financial difficulties and to gain other political objectives (such as separation of the Rhineland from Germany).

The occupation was met by the Germans with a policy of noncooperation, which had been decided upon only days before the actual invasion. There had been no preparation, but the resistance was to be financed by the German government. Trade unions had strongly urged adoption of the policy. One of their spokesmen had argued: "If civil servants and workers stop work whenever the invaders appear, and the employers refuse to fulfill the demands of the Franco-Belgian commissions, it should be possible to deprive the commissions and military forces of the means of carrying out their tasks."

Actual noncooperation against the invasion forces developed gradually. The means included the refusal to obey orders of the occupation forces; nonviolent acts of defiance; the refusal of mine owners to serve the invaders; massive demonstrations at courts during trials of resisters; the refusal of German policemen to salute foreign officials; the refusal of German workers to run the railroads for the French; the dismantling of railroad equipment; the refusal of shopkeepers to sell to foreign soldiers; the refusal of ordinary people, even when hungry, to use occupation-organized soup kitchens; defiant publication of newspapers in spite of many bans; posting of resistance proclamations and posters; and refusal to mine coal.

Repression was severe. It included such measures as the imposition of a state of siege; the expulsion of resisters into unoccupied Germany; courts-martial; the tolerance of bands of thugs and robbers; imprisonment without trial or trials imposing long prison sentences; whippings; shootings; killings; the seizure of money and personal property; control of the press; billeting of troops in homes and schools; imposition of identity cards; and the issuing of a multitude of repressive regulations. Widespread food shortages as a consequence of resistance and repression resulted in severe hunger.

Resistance was complicated by various types of sabotage, including demolitions, which sometimes killed occupation personnel. This sabotage was associated with spies, informers, and assassinations of suspected informers. Demolitions also tended to reduce the international shift of sympathy toward Germany. The Prussian Minister of the Interior Severing, the trade unions, and the population of the occupied area for the most part strongly disapproved of the sabotage by outsiders, which upset the previous unity of the resistance. The sabotage also led to severe reprisals and punishments, both official and spontaneous by angry occupation soldiers. One such measure was the ban on road traffic. Widespread unemployment and hunger were severe problems along with continuing extraordinary inflation. The unity of resistance, and to a large extent even the will to resist, was finally broken.

On September 26, the German government called off the noncooperation campaign, but the sufferings of the population increased. Complex negotiations occurred. Germany finally stabilized the currency, while facing a series of Communist and extreme right-wing insurrections and attempted coups in several of the *Länder*.

Belgians widely protested against their government's actions. Some French people became advocates for the Germans, called *advocats des boches*. Toward the end of 1923, Poincaré admitted to the French National Assembly that his policies had failed. Germany could not claim victory, but the invaders finally withdrew, and the Rhineland was not detached from Germany. The invaders had achieved neither their economic nor their political objectives.

Britain and the United States intervened and secured a restructuring of reparations payments. The Dawes Plan was developed to deal with reparations, occupation costs, and German financial solvency, and provided a loan to Germany—all on the assumption that Germany would remain united.

Occupation forces were all withdrawn by June 1925.

Czechoslovakia, 1968–1969

Civil unrest created serious problems for Soviet hegemony in Eastern Europe in the decades following the Second World War, at times threatening Soviet control in several countries. This took various forms, both nonviolent (strikes, parades, defiant demonstrations, and seizure of control by the populace) and violent (as in rioting and even military action). Among the most significant cases of civilian struggle were the democratization movement in Czechoslovakia in 1968 and the Czech-Slovak national defense resistance of 1968–1969.

The 1968–1969 Czechoslovak case is a most unusual one, and constitutes perhaps the most significant attempt thus far to improvise civilian struggle for national defense purposes. Ultimately, the result was defeat, but not quickly. The first week of resistance was a most remarkable application of noncooperation and defiance. Even after that, for eight months, the Czechs and Slovaks prevented Soviet officials from achieving their political objective, namely, a regime responsive to Soviet wishes. It has been reported that Soviet officials had originally expected military resistance and had estimated they could crush it, install a puppet regime, and then withdraw, all within a few days.

The Soviet leaders thought that invasion by the nearly one-half million Warsaw Pact troops would crush the Czechoslovak army and leave the population in confusion and defeat. The invasion would make possible a coup d'état to replace the Dubček reform regime. Accordingly, as soon as possible, several of the important Czechoslovak leaders were kidnapped by the KGB, including Alexander Dubček, the Communist Party's First Secretary, Prime Minister Oldrich Černik, and National Assembly President Josef Smrkovsky and National Front Chairman František Kriegel. The President of the Republic, Ludvik Svoboda, was held under house arrest.

However, this did not signal a Czechoslovak defeat. Had Czechoslovak leaders decided to resist militarily, their army almost certainly would have been quickly overwhelmed by the immensely larger Warsaw Pact invasion troops. Instead, Czechoslovak officials had given emergency orders for the troops to stay in their barracks and a very different type of resistance was waged.

The particular character of this nonviolent resistance caused serious logistical and morale problems among the invading troops. Reports indicated that it was necessary to replace large portions of the original invasion force within a short period, some within a few days.

Owing to resistance at several strategic political points, a collaborationist government was prevented. Resistance began in the early hours of the invasion as employees of the government news agency refused to issue a press release stating that certain Czechoslovak Communist Party and government leaders had requested the invasion. President Svoboda refused to sign a document presented to him by a group of Stalinist Communists. A clandestine defense radio network called for peaceful resistance, reported on resistance activities, and convened several official bodies that opposed the invasion.

Government officials, party leaders, and organizations denounced the invasion and the National Assembly demanded release of the arrested leaders and the immediate withdrawal of the foreign troops. During the first week, the defense radio network created many forms of noncooperation and opposition and shaped others. It convened the Extraordinary Fourteenth Party Congress, called one-hour general strikes, asked rail workers to slow the transport of Russian communications-tracking and jamming equipment, and discouraged collaboration. The radio argued the futility of violent resistance and the wisdom of nonviolent struggle. It was impossible for the Soviets to find sufficient collaborators to set up their puppet regime.

Although totally successful militarily, Soviet officials found they could not control the country. In the face of unified civilian resistance and the increasing demoralization of their troops, the Soviet leaders flew President Svoboda to Moscow for negotiations, but once there Svoboda insisted on the presence of the arrested Czechoslovak leaders.

A compromise—which was probably a major strategic mistake— was worked out, legitimizing the presence of Soviet troops and sacrificing some of the Czechoslovak reforms. Many of the basic reforms were maintained, however, and the reform group was returned to Prague to their official positions. The general population saw the compromise as a defeat and for a week would not accept it.

Despite weaknesses and compromises, the reform regime and many of the reforms were maintained from August until the following April

when some anti-Soviet rioting provided the pretext for intensified Soviet pressure. This time the Czechoslovak officials capitulated, ousting
the Dubček reform group from party and government positions and
replacing them with the hard-line Husak regime.

The Soviet officials had been forced to shift from their initial use of
military means to gradual political pressures and manipulations, and
had experienced an eight-month delay in gaining their basic objective.
Had full Soviet control been held off for eight months by Czechoslovak
military resistance against such overwhelming odds, the struggle
would have been classed with the Battle of Thermopylae, in which a
small number of Greeks fought to the last man against an immensely
superior Persian army.

The nature and accomplishments of the Czechoslovak defense are
already forgotten by many and, when noted, are frequently distorted.
The defense struggle ultimately failed as a result of capitulation by
Czechoslovak officials, not defeated resistance. But it had held off full
Soviet control for eight months—from August to April—something
that would have been impossible by military means.

All this was done without preparation and training, much less contingency planning. This accomplishment in these highly unfavorable
circumstances suggests, despite the final defeat, that refined, prepared,
and trained nonviolent struggle for actual *defense* may have a power
potential even greater than that of military means.

A Basis for Systematic Development

Such cases as those described and cited in this chapter may provide
the basis for systematic development of a new type of defense capable
of deterring and defending against foreign invasions and internal usurpations.

Up to now, this type of action has been an underdeveloped political
technique. It has been as unrefined as was military action five thousand
or so years ago. As indicated earlier, the participants in nonviolent
struggles have always lacked the prior organization, preparation, improved weaponry, training, and in-depth knowledge of past conflicts
and strategic principles that military practitioners have had for thousands of years. Only conscious efforts to improve the weaponry, organization, training, and strategy of military action multiplied its combat
effectiveness and destructive capacities.

No such efforts have yet been put into civilian struggle. In spite of
this major disadvantage, the practitioners of nonviolent struggle for

national defense have achieved impressive results. We need now to give attention to the question of how so much has been achieved and to whether—and if so, how—a more effective policy of prepared deterrence and defense, drawing in part on the above prototypes, might be created for the future.

Notes

For further analysis and information about points made in this chapter, see Gene Sharp, *Social Power and Political Freedom* (Boston: Porter Sargent, 1980), pp. 263–284, and Gene Sharp, *The Politics of Nonviolent Action* (Boston: Porter Sargent, 1973), pp. 63–105.

The discussion of "defensive defense" presented here contains only the most common features of the numerous proposals in this area. Key advocates of this approach include Horst Afheldt, Anders Boserup, Norbert Hannig, Jochen Löser, Albrecht von Müller, and Lutz Unterseher. For introductory reviews of this approach, see Jonathan Dean, "Alternative Defence: Answer to NATO's Central Front Problems?" *International Affairs*, vol. 64, no. 1 (Winter 1987/1988), pp. 61–88, and Stephen J. Flanagan, "Nonprovocative and Civilian-Based Defenses," in Joseph S. Nye, Jr., Graham T. Allison, and Albert Carnesale, editors, *Fateful Visions: Avoiding Nuclear Catastrophe* (Cambridge, Mass.: Ballinger Publishing Co., 1988), pp. 93–109. See also Frank Barnaby and Egbert Boeker, "Defence Without Offence—Non-nuclear Defence for Europe" (Bradford, England: University of Bradford, Peace Studies Paper No. 8, 1982). Major publications in the field include Horst Afheldt, *Defensive Verteidigung* (Reinbek, Hamburg: Rowohlt Taschenbuch Verlag, 1983); Anders Boserup, "Non-Offensive Defense in Europe," (University of Copenhagen; Centre of Peace and Conflict Research, Working Paper No. 5, 1985); Norbert Hannig, "Verteidigung ohne zu Bedrohen," (Universität Stuttgart: Arbeitsgruppe Friedensforschung und Europäische Sicherheit, Paper No. 5, 1986); Hans-Heinrich Nolte and Wilhelm Nolte, *Ziviler Widerstand und Autonome Abwehr* (Baden-Baden: Nomos Verlag, 1984); Lutz Unterseher, *Defending Europe: Toward a Stable Deterrent* (Bonn: Studiengruppe Alternative Sicherheitspolitik, 1986).

For discussion of "defensive defense" in the context of Swiss defense policy, see Dietrich Fischer, "Invulnerability Without Threat: The Swiss Concept of General Defense," in Burns H. Weston, editor, *Toward Nuclear Disarmament and Global Security—A Search for Alternatives* (Boulder, Colo.: Westview Press, 1984), pp. 504–532.

For a presentation of "defensive defense" as applied to Britain's defense, see Alternative Defence Commission, *Defence Without the Bomb* (London and New York: Taylor and Francis, 1983).

The quotation from Lenin is from "Political Report of the Central Committee of the Russian Communist Party (Bolsheviks)," delivered March 27, 1922, at the Eleventh Congress of the Russian Communist Party (Bolsheviks), in *V. I. Lenin: Selected Works in Three Volumes* (New York: International Publishers, 1967), vol. 3, pp. 692–693.

The account of resistance to the Kapp Putsch is based on Wilfred Harris Crook, *The General Strike* (Chapel Hill, N.C.: University of North Carolina Press, 1931), pp. 496–527; Donald Goodspeed, *The Conspirators* (New York: Viking, 1962), pp. 108–188; Erich Eyck, *A History of the Weimar Republic* (Cambridge, Mass.: Harvard University Press, 1962), vol. 1, pp. 129–160; Karl Roloff (pseud.: Karl Ehrlich), "Den Ikkevoldelige Modstand: den Kvalte Kapp-Kupet," in K. Ehrlich, N. Lindberg, and G. Jacobsen, *Kamp Uden Vaaben* (Copenhagen: Levin & Munksgaard, Einar Munksgaard, 1937), pp. 194–213; and John Wheeler-Bennett, *The Nemesis of Power* (New York: St. Martin's Press, 1953), pp. 63–82. See also Sharp, *The Politics of Nonviolent Action*, pp. 40–41 and 79–81.

The account of resistance to the coup d'état in French Algeria is based upon that of Adam Roberts, "Civil Resistance to Military Coups," *Journal of Peace Research* (Oslo), vol. XII, no. 1 (1975), pp. 19–36. All quotations are from that source.

The description of the Ruhr struggle is based on that of Wolfgang Sternstein, "The *Ruhrkampf* of 1923," in Adam Roberts, editor, *Civilian Resistance as a National Defense* (Harmondsworth, England, and Baltimore, Md.: Penguin Books, 1969), pp. 128–161.

The account of Czechoslovak resistance is based on Robert Littell, editor, *The Czech Black Book* (New York: Praeger, 1969); Robin Remington, editor, *Winter in Prague* (Cambridge, Mass: M.I.T. Press, 1969); Philip Windsor and Adam Roberts, *Czechoslovakia 1968* (New York: Columbia University Press, 1969), and Vladimir Horsky, *Prag 1968: Systemveränderung und Systemverteidigung* (Stuttgart: Ernst Klett Verlag and Munich: Kösel-Verlag, 1975). See also H. Gordon Skilling, *Czechoslovakia's Interrupted Revolution* (Princeton, N.J.: Princeton University Press, 1976).

Two

Tapping the Sources of Power

Unexpected Capacities

How, Except by Accident or under the most exceptional circumstances, could the cases of nonviolent struggle against usurpations and aggression surveyed in the previous chapter have happened? Is there any significance to such events beyond recording for history what occurred in those specific times and places? Or, is it possible that those cases are expressions of a general type of action that has wider relevance?

Other questions quickly arise. Could nonviolent struggle succeed against dictatorships in the future and, if so, how? Could people using this technique really prevent the rise of new systems of oppression? Could a whole society successfully develop and apply a defense policy based on this technique to deter and defeat coups d'état and foreign aggression?

To most people, it seems to be a strange, if not absurd, idea that a population could—without armies, tanks, planes, bombs, and rockets—demolish a dictatorship, make impotent invading armies, block an unconstitutional seizure of the state, and defeat aggressors.

It is no stranger an idea, however, than one that existed in the minds of only a very few scientists in the 1930s. Certain tiny, previously unseen, pieces of matter called "atoms," it was hypothesized, contained a great power potential that could be tapped to produce an explosive capacity unprecedented in human history. The validity of that idea may seem obvious today, but in 1939 most people with "common sense" would have dismissed it, on both the Nazi and Allied sides. There had been no prototypes of such weapons, no small-scale experiments even by the most barbarous, or technically advanced, of aggressors.

Had it not been for the special circumstances of that war, the notion of turning millions of tiny atoms into bombs might have indefinitely remained only the strange conception of a few intellectuals. However, in response to a grave international crisis, vast human and material resources were made available to scientists and technicians in an attempt to transform the power potential of tiny atoms into the world's most devastating weaponry. The consequences are well known.

An insight into political power exists that may have comparably extreme but beneficial consequences. Thus far it has been tapped only to a limited degree. The insight is that a power potential is inherent in societies that can be harnessed and skillfully applied to destroy oppression and tyranny and to deter and defeat aggression so effectively that military weaponry will no longer be needed. In coming years and decades this power potential is likely to have more significant consequences in politics and international conflict than almost anyone has imagined. This is the power potential that was utilized, in very limited degrees, in the cases outlined in the first chapter.

As will be argued in the following chapters, this power potential can be refined, and its effectiveness greatly increased. This enhanced power capacity can then be applied in future acute conflicts, and will likely prove capable of providing both deterrence and defense, without either the weapons of mass destruction or the vast conventional military arsenals that today lack the capacity to *defend*.

In the four cases surveyed in the previous chapter, the populations were not in fact helpless and unarmed. They were, indeed, "armed," but with *other* weapons—psychological, social, economic, and political ones. These weapons were able to strike at the very sources of the usurpers' or aggressors' power. This largely accounts for the fighting capacity of those nonviolent struggles.

The reason why movements of noncooperation and defiance have been at times able to depose once powerful rulers is that such movements strike at the Achilles heel of all governments: they are dependent on the people and the society they rule. Withdrawal of popular and institutional cooperation with aggressors and dictators diminishes, and may sever, the availability of the sources of power on which all rulers depend. Without availability of those sources, the rulers' power weakens and finally dissolves. This is the essence of the insight into political power presented in this chapter.

Dependent Rulers

It is an obvious, simple, but often neglected insight of great theoretical and practical significance that the power wielded by individuals and groups in the highest positions of command and decision in any government—whom we shall for brevity call *rulers*—is not intrinsic to them. They are not born with it, they do not possess it, and they do not personally apply it. Rather, they are able to use such power only as long as it is made available to them.

By "political power" we mean the totality of all influences and pressures, including sanctions (or punishments), available for use in efforts to determine and implement policies for a political society. Political power may be possessed by governments, the state, institutions, opposition movements, and other groups. Such power may be directly applied, or may be maintained as a reserve capacity. Power is therefore present, for example, in negotiations as well as in war. Power in conflicts is wielded by both the winning and losing sides. Political power may be measured by the relative ability to apply pressures, to control a situation, people, and institutions, and to mobilize people and institutions to accomplish some purpose.

Rulers are not omnipotent, nor do they possess self-generating power. By its very nature, political power must come from outside the persons of the rulers. Alone, rulers have neither the physical nor the intellectual capacities to accomplish everything they wish. If rulers are to wield political power, they must be recognized as possessing authority, be able to direct the behavior of other people, draw on large resources, both human and material, direct bureaucracies in the administration of their policies, and command organizations of repression or combat. The availability of each of these sources is dependent on the cooperation and obedience of the population and of the many groups and institutions of the society to be ruled. That means that these components are not automatically at the disposal of the would-be rulers.

Full cooperation, obedience, and support will increase the availability of the needed sources of power and, consequently, the power capacity of the rulers. On the other hand, restricting or withdrawing cooperation will directly and indirectly reduce or sever the availability of the required sources of power. Much like the flow of water from a faucet is controlled by turns of the valve, cooperation and noncooperation can control the availability of the resources required to rule.

Naturally, rulers are sensitive to the imposition of limits on their capacity to do as they like. They may well see danger in the spread of such ideas. Rulers are therefore likely to threaten and punish those who disobey, strike, or fail to cooperate, with the aim of breaking their defiance. However, that is not the end of the story.

If, despite repression, the sources of power can be restricted, withheld, or severed for sufficient time, the initial results may be uncertainty and confusion within the regime. That is likely to be followed by a perceptible weakening of the rulers' power. Over time, the result of withholding the sources of power will eventually be the paralysis and impotence of the regime, or even in severe cases its disintegration. The rulers' power will die, slowly or rapidly, from political starvation.

This same principle of political power was expressed by Etienne de la Boétie in 1548. Speaking of the tyrant, he wrote, "He who abuses you so has only two eyes, has but two hands, one body, and has naught but what has the least man of the great and infinite number of your cities, except for the advantage you give him to destroy you." It was from the suffering people, Boétie argued, that the tyrant gained everything he needed to rule: legitimacy, money, aides, soldiers, even the young women with whom he spent his nights. Consequently, Boétie concluded, if tyrants "are given nothing, if they are not obeyed, without fighting, without striking a blow, they remain naked and undone, and do nothing further, just as the root, having no soil or food, the branch withers and dies."

Identifying the Sources of Power

Political power emerges from the interaction of all or several of the following sources:

Authority. The extent and intensity of the rulers' authority, or legitimacy, among the subjects is a crucial factor affecting the rulers' power. How widely, deeply, and firmly do the people believe in the rulers' right to govern them? If the rulers' authority is strong, other sources of power are more likely to be made available, and the need for threat or use of sanctions to enforce obedience and cooperation is likely to be small.

Human resources. The power of rulers is affected by the number of persons and groups which obey, cooperate, or provide special assistance; by the proportion of those persons in the general population; and by the extent, forms, and power of their organizations. How many people and what institutions are helping, or are refusing to help?

Skills and knowledge. The rulers' power is also affected by the skills, knowledge, and abilities of persons and groups who are willing to obey and assist the rulers, as well as by their ability to supply the rulers' needs. Do they possess the capacities which the rulers require? What is the extent of the rulers' dependency on their skills, knowledge, and abilities?

Intangible factors. Psychological and ideological factors, emotions and beliefs, are also important in supporting the rulers. These factors include habits and attitudes toward obedience and submission, and the presence or absence of a common faith, ideology, or sense of mission. If these factors are strong, the rulers will likely find other sources of power more readily available, whereas if the intangible factors are weak or absent, the availability of other sources of power will be more problematical.

Material resources. The degree to which rulers control—directly or indirectly—property, natural resources, financial resources, the economic system, the means of communication and of transportation helps to determine the limits of the rulers' power. Are these material resources readily available to serve the rulers' objectives, or are they not?

Sanctions. The final source of the power of rulers is the type and extent of sanctions (or punishments) available to them. Such sanctions may be threatened or applied both against the rulers' own subjects, when they are disobedient or noncooperative, and against the countries and forces of foreign rulers with whom they are in conflict. These questions therefore arise: What pressures, punishments, and means of struggle are at the disposal of rulers in such situations? Are these readily, reliably, and fully available, or are they restricted?

It is almost always a matter of the *degree* to which some or all of these sources of power are present. Only rarely, if ever, are all of them fully available to rulers or completely absent. The availability of such sources is subject to constant variation. These changes bring about increases or decreases in the rulers' power. The degree, extent, and duration of the rulers' power is determined by the extent to which rulers have unrestricted access to these sources.

Dependency on the Governed

A closer examination of these sources of the rulers' power will indicate that they depend greatly or completely (varying with the situation) upon the obedience and cooperation of the governed. Let us look further at the consequences of the withdrawal of these sources.

If the subjects deny the rulers' right to rule, they are withdrawing the general agreement, or group consent, that makes the existing government possible. This loss of authority, or legitimacy, sets in motion the weakening or disintegration of the rulers' power. Where the loss is extreme, the existence of that particular government is threatened. The denial of authority to internal usurpers and to foreign aggressors is therefore a key element in a civilian-based defense struggle aimed at preventing the establishment of a new government of internal or foreign oppressors. Once the population has denied the rulers' authority, it is likely to restrict its cooperation, obedience, and assistance, or refuse them entirely. Disobedience and noncooperation are serious problems for any regime.

Every ruler needs the skill, knowledge, advice, labor, and administrative ability of a significant portion of the subjects. The more extensive and detailed the rulers' control is, the more such assistance the rulers will require. Contributions to the rulers' power will range, for example, from the specialized knowledge of a technical expert, the research endeavors of a scientist, and the organizational abilities of a department head to the assistance of typists, factory workers, computer specialists, communication technicians, transportation workers, and farmers. Both the economic and the political systems operate because of the contributions of many individuals, organizations, and subgroups.

The rulers' power depends on the continual availability of all this assistance, not only from individual experts, officials, employees, and the like, but from the subsidiary organizations and institutions that comprise the system as a whole. These may include departments, bureaus, branches, committees, and the like. Just as individuals and independent groups may refuse to cooperate, so too these subsidiary organizations may refuse to provide sufficient help to maintain the rulers' position and to implement the rulers' policies.

If the multitude of the subjects and institutions of the society that have previously assisted the rulers in providing the various sources of power come to reject the rulers' authority, then the availability of those sources is threatened. The population and institutions that once assisted reliably, now may instead only carry out the rulers' wishes inefficiently, may even abrogate unto themselves certain decisions, or may flatly refuse to continue their past assistance, cooperation, and obedience to the rulers.

Without conscientious and reliable work by many employees, the skills, knowledge, and human resources crucial to a functioning administration and bureaucracy will not be present. Without dependable participation of numerous laborers, farmers, technicians, managers, transportation workers, communication employees, and researchers, the economic system will not function effectively. Unless the police and soldiers dependably obey the orders from their officers, the institutions of repression will not be able to act reliably against resisters.

Refusal to do what one is told is not dependent upon careful study of the writings of Henry David Thoreau or Mohandas K. Gandhi. Very young children, as well as many youths and adults, become very skilled in disobedience and noncooperation quite naturally. It is a phenomenon widely recognized in our society, communicated in the old saying, "You can lead a horse to water, but you can't make it drink." Rather than being necessarily based on a profound understanding of political theory, an acceptance of certain religious precepts, or achievement of a higher level of moral development, the capacity to disobey and refuse political cooperation is simply rooted in our human propensity to be stubborn when it suits us. However, when applied by masses of people acting collectively for a cause in which they believe, the action becomes powerful because it coincides with the type of action prescribed by an understanding of the basic nature of political power.

Repression Insufficient

Rulers will neither be pleased by nor will easily acquiesce in the face of defiance. Indeed, as noted above, the withdrawal of consent by noncooperation will most likely be seen as a severe threat. In the face of serious political unrest, if the regime is not prepared to make changes to meet popular demands, it will have to place increased reliance on enforcement.

In order to regain or ensure the assistance, obedience, and cooperation they require, officials may threaten or apply punishments, which may include beatings, imprisonments, torture, and executions. Such sanctions are usually possible despite widespread dissatisfaction with the regime because very often one segment of the populace remains loyal and willing to help the regime maintain itself and to carry out its policies. In such a case, rulers may use the loyal subjects as police or soldiers to inflict punishments on the remainder of the people. Sanctions, however, will still not then be the determining force in maintaining that regime for two reasons. The ruling group (foreign or domestic) will still be united by something other than sanctions, such as religious belief, economic self-interest, ideology, belief in their mission, and the like. Furthermore, the rulers' ability to apply sanctions at home or abroad arises from and depends upon a significant degree of help from the subjects themselves.

Sanctions *are* important in maintaining the rulers' political power—especially in crises. That does *not* mean, however, that those punishments will always succeed in restoring submission and obedience, either in the long or short run.

Even if the rulers' punishments do at first result in a degree of outward conformity, that will be insufficient to produce a lasting effect. Rulers need more than grudging, outward forms of compliance. Forced submission will often lead to inefficiency in carrying out duties, if not to deliberate slowdowns. As long as the extent and intensity of the rulers' authority among these subjects is limited, submission induced by threats and punishments will inevitably be inadequate to ensure lasting full power capacity.

Even in the short-run, the rulers cannot be assured that their punishments against a resisting population will necessarily succeed in restoring submission, nor even that the capacity to apply sanctions will always be fully available to them. Even when the repressors' sanctions

are applied reliably against a defiant population, they are not necessarily effective in producing renewed obedience and cooperation.
Whether punishments are or are not effective depends on the subjects'
particular pattern of submission. This hinges not only on how fully the
population in normal times obeys orders and instructions. It also depends on whether at that particular time and under those specific conditions the subjects are prepared to obey and cooperate or whether
they are prepared to continue to defy the rulers *despite* the threatened
or applied punishments.

Even when resisters are confronted with punishments, there is a role
for an act of will, for choice. They can choose to obey, thus avoiding the
sanctions threatened for disobedience. Or, they can choose to disobey
and risk receiving the threatened sanctions. This is not necessarily a
matter of great political sophistication. Many headstrong young children, as well as rebellious teenagers, repeatedly court risks of punishments, albeit milder ones.

If people are unwilling to comply except for the prospect of punishment, the sanctions in order to be effective must be *feared*. Their consequences must be seen as more undesirable than the expected results of
obedience. Threatened or inflicted punishments only produce obedience and submission when they affect the subjects' minds and emotions, when the subjects fear the sanctions and are unwilling to suffer
them. Sanctions, by themselves, do not produce the desired results: a
beaten protester may return the next day, a jailed striker still does not
work, and an executed mutineer can never again carry out orders. Punishments only succeed if they increase submission to a degree adequate
to accomplish the rulers' objectives.

Importantly, when fear of punishments does *not* control the subjects'
minds, repression is unlikely to succeed. As in wars, the prospect of
physical injury and death does not cause soldiers at the front to flee or
to surrender. If the "fighting forces"—military or civilian, violent or
nonviolent—believe in their cause sufficiently, they are likely to continue the struggle regardless of the danger to them individually. In
such conditions, repression may even aggravate the alienation of the
population against the regime and increase the numbers of resisters.

The rulers' power is also vulnerable in another way. As we noted,
the ability to impose sanctions derives from the obedience and cooperation of at least some subjects. Arrests, imprisonments, beatings, and
other forms of repression require action by police, army, paramilitary,
or other forces, and often some type of assistance from the general population. The agents of repression must be willing to inflict such punishments reliably. In some circumstances that will not be the case.

The police, soldiers, and the like, may no longer accept that the past or would-be rulers currently have any right to give such orders. Or, the members of such forces may actually be, or become, sympathetic to the cause of the resisting population, and hence hesitate to punish people who are acting on behalf of that cause. The police and troops may intentionally carry out orders inefficiently when they think they have at least to *appear* to obey their superiors. Also, the experience of police and troops of inflicting violent repression against *nonviolent* resisters has, in a variety of circumstances, reduced their own willingness to obey. At times, the result has even been large-scale disaffection, disguised disobedience, or open mutiny against orders to continue brutal repression of nonviolent people. This is one important reason why maintenance of nonviolent discipline, discussed in Chapter Three, is so important.

All three of those important factors—denial of authority, sympathy with the resisters' cause, and distaste for committing violence against nonviolent people—can be consciously influenced in ways that could significantly weaken, if not dissolve, the rulers' power.

The Possibility of Collective Resistance

If the rulers' power is to be controlled by withdrawing help and obedience, widespread noncooperation and disobedience must be maintained in the face of repression aimed at forcing renewed submission. Once there has been a major reduction of, or an end to, the subjects' fear, and once there is a willingness to suffer sanctions as the price of change, large-scale disobedience and noncooperation become possible.

Such action then becomes politically significant, and the rulers' will is thwarted in proportion to the number of disobedient subjects and the degree of the rulers' dependence upon them. The answer to the problem of apparently uncontrollable political power may, therefore, lie in learning how to initiate large-scale withdrawal of cooperation and how to maintain it despite repression.

The theory that political power derives from violence, and that victory necessarily goes to the side with the greater capacity for violence, is false. Instead, the choice to disobey, the will to defy, and the ability to resist become extremely important in securing victory over oppressors, tyrants, and aggressors who have almost unlimited capacity to destroy and kill.

In July 1943, Hitler admitted that "ruling the people in the conquered regions is, I might say, of course a psychological problem. One cannot rule by force alone. True, force is decisive, but it is equally important to have this psychological something which the animal trainer also needs to be master of his beast. They must be convinced that we are the victors."

What, then, if people refuse to accept the militarily successful invaders as their political masters? What if people repudiate the claims of their own military forces that have occupied the capital, arrested or killed elected officials, and declared that the rebellious military forces are the new government? When the general population understands its own potential, rooted in the very nature of political power, these questions raise realistic, if rarely explored, practical options.

Requirements for Implementation

If this insight into political power is to be implemented, the key question becomes *how*. The lack of knowledge of how to act against existing oppressive rulers and how to prevent the rise of new ones has been one of the most important reasons why people have not more often acted effectively on this insight and long since abolished tyranny and oppression. Action on this insight has at least two major requirements.

First, the people must actively express their rejection of the tyrannical government by refusing to cooperate. This refusal may take many forms. Few of these will be easy, many will be dangerous, and each will require effort, courage, and intelligence.

Second, there must be group or mass action. When the ruling minority is unified and well organized but the ruled majority is divided and lacks independent organization, the people are usually weak and incapable of collective opposition. They can be dealt with one by one. Effective action requires *collective* resistance and defiance. Ordinarily, the sources of the rulers' power are threatened significantly only when assistance, cooperation, and obedience are withheld by large numbers of subjects at the same time, that is, by social groups and institutions.

For example, sermons by a dissident priest may affect only a few devoted local parishioners, while denunciation of the regime by the entire church as illegitimate, speaking to the whole nation, can lead to the government's collapse. A handful of workers who walk off their jobs in protest may simply be fired, while a well-organized strike by a solid union of many thousands may force major concessions. A few government employees who ignore orders may hardly be noticed, while noncooperation by most of the bureaucracy can make the executive impotent.

Noncooperation and disobedience by organizations and institutions, as distinct from isolated individuals, is therefore essential. The ability of such bodies to withhold the sources of power they supply is consequently pivotal.

The Structural Basis of Popular Control

The ability of the population to act collectively to control its rulers will be highly influenced by the condition of the society's non-state organizations and institutions, since it is through these bodies that people can act collectively. These non-state organizations and institutions are the loci of power. They are the "places" in the society in which power is located, converges, or is expressed.

The precise form and nature of these loci of power varies from society to society, and from situation to situation within the same society. They are, however, likely to include such social groups and institutions as families, social classes, religious groups, cultural and nationality groups, occupational groups, economic groups, villages and towns, cities, provinces and regions, smaller governmental bodies, voluntary organizations, and political parties. Most often they are traditional, established, formal social groups and institutions. Sometimes, however, loci of power may be less formally organized. They may even be created or revitalized in the process of achieving some objective or in the development of the resistance struggle itself.

In any case, the status of organizations and institutions as loci of power will be determined by their capacity to act independently, to wield effective power, and to regulate the power of other loci or the power of the rulers commanding the state apparatus.

This complex of independent units and power relationships provides the "structural" basis for potential control of rulers and would-be rulers. The "structural condition" of the society as a whole is determined by three factors. The first is the extent and vitality of these loci of power. This includes whether such independent groups and institutions exist, their number, the degree of their internal strength and vitality, how centralized or decentralized they are, and their internal decision-making processes.

The second factor comprises the relationships among these independent groups and institutions of the society. Can these loci of power work together for common objectives? Can they coordinate their planning and action?

The third is the relationship between these loci and the rulers. Are the loci really capable of independent action vis-à-vis the rulers, that is, capable of disobeying and not cooperating with them, thereby restricting or severing sources of the rulers' power? Or is the degree of their actual independence of action quite limited?

The structural condition will set the broad boundaries of the rulers' potential power, beyond which they may not go without structural changes or without increased authority, voluntary acceptance, and active assistance from the subjects and their institutions. If power is highly decentralized among strong and vital independent institutions, that condition, in emergencies, will greatly strengthen the capacity of the subjects and their institutions collectively to withdraw the sources of the rulers' or would-be rulers' power in order to impose popular control.

The Structural Basis of Freedom

When power is effectively diffused throughout the society among strong loci, the rulers' power is most likely subjected to controls and limits, thus enabling the society to resist oppression, usurpation, and aggression. This condition is associated with political "freedom." When, on the other hand, such loci have been seriously weakened or their independence of action has been destroyed, when the subjects are all equally impotent and the society's power has become highly centralized, then the rulers' power will most likely be uncontrolled. This condition is associated with "tyranny." It is no accident that past totalitarian systems have attempted either to eliminate all independent groups or to subject them to full control by the party or state.

Ultimately, therefore, freedom is not something that rulers "give" their subjects. Nor, in the long run, do the formal institutional structures and procedures of the government (as, for example, may be laid out in the constitution) by themselves determine the degree of freedom or the limits of the rulers' power. A society may in fact be more free or more oppressed than the formal constitutional or legal arrangements would indicate. Instead, the extent and intensity of the rulers' power and the actual degree of freedom of the society will be set by the strength of the subjects and the condition of the institutions of the whole society. The rulers' power and the degree of the society's freedom may, in turn, be expanded or contracted by the interplay between the actions of the rulers and those of the subjects: some rulers may choose not to be as oppressive as the structural condition permits, and other rulers may receive more support than the structural condition requires, making them more powerful.

Increases in the rulers' power are directly or indirectly determined, on the one hand, by the willingness of the subjects to accept the rulers, to obey, to cooperate and to carry out their orders and wishes. On the other hand, reductions in the rulers' power are determined by the subjects' unwillingness to accept the rulers, coupled with their ability to disobey, to withhold cooperation, to defy orders, and to refuse demands made upon them.

The degree of liberty or tyranny in any political society is, it follows, largely a reflection of the relative determination of the subjects to be free, of their willingness and ability to organize themselves to live in freedom and, very importantly, their ability to resist any efforts to dominate or enslave them. In other words, the population can use the society itself as the means to establish and defend its freedom. Social power, not technological means of destruction, is the strongest guarantor of human freedom.

Societal Origins of Defense

These insights into the nature of political power and the means of imposing limits on—or dissolving—the rulers' power are highly relevant to the problem of how to provide effective defense of the society against both internal usurpers and foreign aggressors. They indicate that both the general population and the society's institutions can play key roles in providing an effective defense.

The population and institutions can do this by refusing to grant the acceptance, submission, and cooperation that attackers require. The principle behind these actions, as we have seen, is simple: restriction of the sources of the power—authority, human resources, skills and knowledge, intangible factors, material resources, and sanctions— weakens, while their severance disintegrates, the rulers' power.

This insight opens the way for the defenders to combat the attackers by directly applying the internal strength of the society against the attack. By maintaining its own standards of legitimacy, its own way of life, the autonomy of its institutions and its constitutional principles, the society can neutralize an attack and maintain itself. By mobilizing the full power of the society not to cooperate with efforts to achieve the attackers' goals, the society can defeat the attackers' efforts to force the society to provide any economic, political, or ideological gains. Psychological, social, economic, and political pressures and sanctions of the whole society can be used to produce final defeat of the attack by making ineffective and unreliable the attackers' own forces of administration and repression.

Under certain circumstances, various sections of the state apparatus that have loyally served past rulers may become less reliable in conflict situations. These groupings may sometimes be whole governmental institutions—such as the state bank, the supreme court, or provincial governments. At other times they may be groupings within such institutions—such as parts of the bureaucracy and civil service or sections of the police or military forces.

When whole institutions or significant sections of them begin to make their own decisions and act autonomously in defiance of orders from the rulers or would-be rulers, they become unstable elements of a centrally controlled state apparatus. They are then taking on major characteristics of *independent loci* of power in the society. If those disaffected sections of the state apparatus continue this process of increasing their autonomy, they will contribute to the disintegration of that particular state apparatus. This is, of course, a profound threat to the group that is attempting to remain or become "rulers," which the society rejects as despots, usurpers, or aggressors.

This weakening and destruction of the power of attackers is possible without use of destructive military weaponry. When a society is internally strong, committed to its self-determination, and is well prepared to defy attackers and oppressors, then its most effective response to attempts at internal usurpation and foreign aggression is defense by societal power.

In cases of international aggression, efforts to stimulate or capitalize on dissent and opposition in the attackers' homeland and to arouse international political, diplomatic, and economic sanctions against the attackers also become important components of the defense efforts. The ability of the defending society to gain support from the attackers' home base and from the international community will also be influenced in part by that society's previous policies.

In summary, the ability of a population with strong loci of power to resist usurpers and aggressors will be influenced by various factors. These include (1) the relative desire of the populace to resist the attackers, (2) the number, strength, and independence of the society's organizations and institutions, (3) the ability of these loci of power to work together to defend the society, (4) the amount of social power that the loci can independently wield, (5) the sources of power that they control and the attackers' relative need of those sources, (6) the defenders' relative ability to withhold their cooperation despite repression, and (7) their skill in applying nonviolent struggle effectively.

If the defenders want to resist, have strong independent institutions capable of controlling significant sources of political power, and are able to mount a skillful campaign of noncooperation and defiance, then defense by societal power is a realistic choice to fight the attack. Generalized obstinacy and collective stubbornness are not sufficient, however. Before they begin, people will need to know how to conduct the struggle that will follow their initial act of defiance. They will need to understand the nonviolent technique of action that is based on the insight into political power presented in this chapter. What makes this technique fail and succeed? What is required to produce maximum effectiveness? What options does it provide, and what requirements does it impose? This needed understanding of nonviolent action must include its specific methods, its dynamics of change, requirements for success, and its principles of strategy and tactics.

Notes

For a much more detailed development of this analysis of power and many references, see Gene Sharp, *The Politics of Nonviolent Action* (Boston: Porter Sargent, 1973), pp. 7–62 and Gene Sharp, *Social Power and Political Freedom* (Boston: Porter Sargent, 1980), pp. 21–67. Among the theorists whose insights have been used in the development of those analyses are Auguste Comte, T. H. Green, Errol E. Harris, Etienne de la Boétie, Harold D. Lasswell, John Austin, Baron de Montesquieu, Jean-Jacques Rousseau, William Godwin, Bertrand de Jouvenel, Robert MacIver, Chester I. Barnard, Niccolo Machiavelli, W. A. Rudlin, Max Weber, Herbert Goldhamer, Edward A. Shils, Karl W. Deutsch, Jeremy Bentham, Georg Simmel, E. V. Walter, Franz Neumann, David Hume, Thomas Hobbes, Jacques Maritain, and Alexis de Tocqueville. Specific references to their works are contained in the above cited studies.

On the factors contributing to success or failure in nonviolent struggle, see Sharp, *The Politics of Nonviolent Action*, pp. 726–731, 754–755, and 815–817.

The quotation from Boétie is from Etienne de la Boétie, "Discours de la Servitude Volontaire," in *Oeuvres Completes d'Etienne de la Boétie* (Paris: J. Rouam & Cie., 1892), p. 12 and pp. 8–11. The translation is by Madeleine Chevalier Emrick. See also Boétie, *Anti-Dictator: The "Discours sur la servitude volontaire" of Etienne de la Boétie*, trans. by Harry Kurz (New York: Columbia University Press, 1942).

The quotation from Hitler is contained in Alexander Dallin, *German Rule in Russia 1941–1945* (New York: St. Martin's, 1957), p. 498.

Three ─────────────────────────

Wielding Power

A Nonviolent Weapons System

IN POLITICAL TERMS, nonviolent action is based on a very simple postulate: people do not always do as they are told, and sometimes they do things that have been forbidden. Subjects may disobey laws they reject. Workers may halt work. The bureaucracy may refuse to carry out instructions. Soldiers and police may inefficiently carry out orders to inflict repression, or may even mutiny.

When these and similar activities happen simultaneously, the rulers' power dissolves as its sources are restricted. The regime disintegrates and the persons who have been "rulers" simply become ordinary human beings. This may be achieved even though the government's military equipment remains intact, its soldiers uninjured, its cities unscathed, the factories and transport systems still fully operational, and the government buildings undamaged. Yet, everything is changed because the human assistance that created and supported the regime's political power has been withdrawn.

How is this insight into power to be translated into action relevant for defense of the society? What methods can defenders use in order to withdraw the sources of power needed by foreign aggressors and internal usurpers? What do they need to do in the face of expected repression? A closer analysis of the technique of nonviolent action may provide some answers.

Nonviolent action is so different from milder, peaceful responses to conflict (such as conciliation and arbitration) that several writers have pointed out that it has instead significant similarities to conventional war. *Nonviolent action is a means of combat, as is war.* It involves the matching of forces and the waging of "battles," requires wise strategy and tactics, employs numerous "weapons," and demands of its "soldiers" courage, discipline, and sacrifice. Nonviolent action may understandably also be called "nonviolent struggle," especially when strong forms of this technique are employed against determined and resourceful opponents who respond with repression and other serious countermeasures.

This view of nonviolent action as a technique of *active* combat is diametrically opposed to the once popular, though uninformed, assertion that no such phenomenon really existed, or that anything "nonviolent" was simple passivity and submission. Other detractors acknowledged the existence of nonviolent action, but argued that, at its strongest, this form of struggle relied on rational persuasion of opponents or on the impact of moral appeals and the "melting of hearts"—both of which were manifestly unlikely to happen in acute conflicts. However, the undeniable power of important nonviolent struggles, especially in the years since 1968—such as the Czech and Slovak resistance, the Solidarity movement in Poland, the Filipino victory over Marcos, the 1989 nonviolent revolutions in East Germany, Czechoslovakia, and Bulgaria—has compelled a degree of recognition even from skeptics.

Nonviolent action is just what it says: *action* that is nonviolent, *not inaction*. This technique consists, not simply of words, but of action in the form of symbolic protests, social, economic, and political noncooperation, and nonviolent intervention. Overwhelmingly, nonviolent action is group or mass action. While certain forms of this technique, especially the symbolic methods, may be regarded as efforts to persuade by action, the other forms, especially those of noncooperation may, if practiced by large numbers, paralyze or even disintegrate the opponents' system.

The motives for using nonviolent action instead of some type of violent action differ widely. In the overwhelming number of past cases nonviolent struggle was selected because it was seen as more likely to succeed than other means. In some situations, previous direct experience with the use of violence, or knowledge of its consequences, has led people to be cautious about using such techniques. ("Violence" here refers to the threat or deliberate infliction of physical injury or death on persons.) Experience with violence may have included riots, violent insurrections, terrorist campaigns, guerrilla warfare, or conventional wars. The prospect of bloody defeat, the probability of immense casualties and vast destruction, or the likely long-term consequences of violence (social distrust, economic decline, increased chances of future military rule, or stimulation of internal violence) have led people to explore nonviolent options. In a relatively few other cases violence has been rejected for religious, ethical, or moral reasons—thus opening the way for the nonviolent technique. In still others, a mixture of practical and principled motives led to a rejection of violence.

Once nonviolent struggle has been selected for use in the conflict, the task for people seeking victory through this form of action is to increase their basic strength and to apply the technique skillfully. Nonviolent action has requirements that need to be fulfilled if it is to be successful. Practitioners of nonviolent action must seek to satisfy these requirements to the maximum of their abilities.

While it is widely assumed that nonviolent action takes longer to succeed than violent struggle, this is not necessarily true. At times, violent struggles have taken many months or years. Look, for example, at the duration of many guerrilla struggles, say in China, Yugoslavia, Algeria, and Vietnam, or the length of various international wars, such as the two world wars. (Remember the Thirty Years War and the Hundred Years War in Europe?) The presumption that military warfare works quickly as a general rule is false, as is the belief that military means offer good chances of success. At least half of the time military efforts are in fact defeated—one side loses. And that does not even consider whether the original *objectives* of the struggle were in fact gained. In cases of military stalemate, neither side wins.

On the other hand, nonviolent struggles have at times not only succeeded (sometimes even dissolving oppressive governments), but have done so quickly. The Kapp Putsch, for example, was defeated in less than five days. The Salvadoran dictator General Maximiliano Hernández Martínez was ousted by a nonviolent insurrection in less than three weeks in April and May 1944. The military dictator Jorge Ubico was removed from the presidency in Guatemala in a struggle that lasted only eleven days in June of that same year. In 1989 the East German, Czechoslovak, and Bulgarian dictatorships collapsed after only a few weeks of large–scale nonviolent resistance in each country.

Not all struggles succeed so quickly, but whether they take days or years, effectiveness depends on the capacity of the users of nonviolent action to stick with the technique they have chosen and to apply it persistently and skillfully. This is not a technique that can produce success if it is thoughtlessly initiated or easily abandoned. Rather, great care is required in planning and strict discipline in implementation if the impact is to be the greatest.

It is dangerous to view nonviolent action as a trivial sideline to the main (most likely violent) action or simply a precursor to some other grand strategy of struggle. Clearly nonviolent action is not a technique that can be advantageous when combined with violence. In fact, that is most dangerous, for, as will be discussed more fully later in this chapter, violence is counterproductive to essential elements of the nonviolent technique. Such violence, frequently in even limited degrees, has had the effect of reducing the numbers of resisters and thereby weakening the strength of their noncooperation. In addition, violence may reduce the impact of the nonviolent character of the movement on the opponents' camp (especially on police and troops) and lessen the degree of sympathy and support from third parties. Violence, therefore, added to a nonviolent struggle, actually weakens, not strengthens, such a movement.

Nonviolent action is a distinctive form of conflict. It employs its own strategies, tactics, and "weapons system." Planned and employed wisely, the technique is capable of offering to its users ways to apply and to mobilize their power potential to a greater degree than does violence.

In order to explore the defensive applications of nonviolent action, it is first necessary to examine the multitude of nonviolent "weapons," or specific methods of action, with which this technique operates. Then, the mechanisms by which nonviolent action produces success need to be explored. Based on this general understanding of the nonviolent technique, attention can then be focused in Chapter Four on the problems of internal usurpation and foreign aggression.

The Methods of Nonviolent Action

Nonviolent action may involve *acts of omission*—that is, people may refuse to perform acts that they usually perform, are expected by custom to perform, or are required by law or regulation to perform; *acts of commission*—that is, people may perform acts that they do not usually perform, are not expected by custom to perform, or are forbidden by law or regulation to perform; or *a combination* of the two.

These acts comprise a multitude of specific means of action or "weapons." Nearly two hundred have been identified to date, and, without doubt, scores or hundreds of additional ones already exist or will emerge in future conflicts. Three broad classes of nonviolent weapons exist within the technique of nonviolent struggle: *nonviolent protest and persuasion, noncooperation,* and *nonviolent intervention.*

Nonviolent Protest and Persuasion

This is a large class of mainly symbolic actions of peaceful opposition or attempted persuasion, extending beyond verbal expression but stopping short of noncooperation or nonviolent intervention. These are the mildest of the nonviolent "weapons." Among these methods are parades, vigils, public speeches, declarations by organizations, renunciations of honors, symbolic public acts, picketing, posters, teach-ins, mourning, and protest meetings.

Their use may simply show that the protesters are *against* or *for* something. The act may be intended primarily to influence the opponents. Alternatively, the act may aim to communicate with the public, onlookers, or third parties, directly or through publicity, in order to arouse attention to and support for the desired change. The act may also be intended primarily to induce the "grievance group"—the persons directly affected by the issue—to take action themselves, such as to participate in a strike or economic boycott. Certain mild methods of this class (such as leafleting) are intended to persuade in order to produce a stronger action (such as an economic boycott) by someone else.

These methods of nonviolent protest and persuasion have been used extremely widely in the forms of distributing leaflets, picketing, carrying posters, or conducting marches. Here are just a few examples. Anti-Nazi pastoral letters were read in German churches on several occasions. The Presidium of the Czechoslovak National Assembly sent a declaration denouncing the Soviet-led invasion of Czechoslovakia and demanding "immediate withdrawal" to the governments and parliaments of the five invading Warsaw Pact countries. A "Memorandum" signed by dozens of Hungary's elite Communist writers and artists in early November 1956 requested the Central Committee of the Communist Party to stop officials from applying "anti-democratic methods which cripple our cultural life" and called for "a free and sincere and healthy and democratic atmosphere imbued with the spirit of popular rule."

During President Wilson's address to Congress on December 4, 1916, five suffragists in the gallery unrolled a banner saying: "MR. PRESIDENT, WHAT WILL YOU DO FOR WOMAN SUFFRAGE?" During the 1963 Buddhist campaign against the Diem regime in South Vietnam, students at the Chu Van An boy's school in Saigon tore down the government flag and hoisted the Buddhist flag. In occupied Poland in 1942 the Germans destroyed all monuments that commemorated Polish heroes or patriotic events. The Poles then made conspicuous detours around those spots and even offered prayers there, to the outrage of German officials.

In Sofia, Bulgaria, Jews organized a protest against planned deportations, which was joined on May 24, 1943, by many non-Jewish Bulgarians. There were clashes with the police and many arrests. Matei Yulzari wrote: "Fearing internal unrest, the Fascist government and the king were forced to give up their plan to send the Jews of Bulgaria to their doom in the death camps." All Jews who were Bulgarian citizens were saved.

In Algiers on August 31, 1962, a crowd of 20,000 gathered in a square to protest the on-going quarrel between the leaders of the newly independent country and to prevent the outbreak of civil war. In Brazil, massive public demonstrations became a major force in the movement of the early 1980s for restoration of civilian government, with strictly nonviolent mass demonstrations at times involving as many as one million and two million people.

On November 4, 1989, at least 500,000 protesters marched through East Berlin demanding free elections, a free press, and civil rights. Some demonstrators posted their demands on the walls of the Council of Ministers building as they filed past. In Prague, on November 25, 1989, one-half million protesters shouting "Shame! Shame! Shame!" gathered to denounce the mere shuffling of the despised Communist leaders as a "trick" intended to subvert reform.

Noncooperation

Most of the methods of nonviolent action involve noncooperation of some type. Noncooperation involves the deliberate discontinuance, restriction, withholding, or defiance of certain existing relationships—social, economic, or political.

People may, for example, totally ignore members of the opposition group. They may refuse to buy certain products, or they may stop work. They may disobey laws they regard as immoral or refuse to pay taxes. Such people struggle by reducing or ceasing their usual cooperation, or by withholding new assistance, or both. This produces a slowing or halting of normal operations. The action may be spontaneous or planned, legal or illegal.

The methods of noncooperation are divided into three main classes: social, economic, and political.

Social noncooperation may involve a refusal to carry on normal social relationships, either specific ones or all types, with persons or groups regarded as having perpetrated some wrong or injustice.

Social boycotts are very well known. During the 1923 *Ruhrkampf*, French and Belgian soldiers and officials were socially boycotted by the Germans. When soldiers entered a tavern for a drink, the German guests would promptly leave. In Denmark during the Second World War, Danes commonly practiced the "cold shoulder" against German soldiers, sometimes looking right through them as though they did not exist.

The methods of social noncooperation also encompass various other forms, including refusal to comply with expected behavior patterns or established practices of the society or the opponent group. Among other similar methods are excommunication, Lysistratic nonaction, suspension of social and sports activities, boycott of social affairs, student strikes, stays-at-home, and the offering of sanctuary.

Economic noncooperation consists of suspension of specific economic relationships or refusal to initiate new ones. Economic forms of noncooperation are much more numerous than those of social noncooperation. This subclass includes both economic boycotts and the strike.

Economic boycotts involve the refusal of certain economic relationships, especially the buying, selling, or handling of goods and services. They may be either *primary* or *secondary* ones. The primary boycott is the direct suspension of dealings with the opponents, such as the refusal of German rail workers to transport coal to France during the 1923 *Ruhrkampf* and the week-long refusal in September 1941 of Prague citizens to buy German-controlled newspapers. The secondary boycott is applied against third parties to induce them to join in the primary boycott against the opponents, such as boycotts of stores in the United States selling boycotted California grapes or boycotted South African products.

Economic boycotts take many forms, including consumers' boycotts, rent withholding, international consumers' boycotts, producers' boycotts, lockouts, refusal to pay debts or interest, withdrawal of bank deposits, and international trade embargoes.

Economic boycotts have been used mainly by labor unions and national liberation movements. Economic boycotts may be conducted by consumers, workers and producers, distributors, owners and managers, holders of financial resources, and governments.

The strike is a refusal to work. It is a collective, deliberate, and normally temporary restriction or suspension of labor designed to exert pressure on others. The issues are usually economic, but not necessarily so. The aim is to produce some change in the relationships of the conflicting groups. The strikers usually make certain demands as a precondition for resuming work. Sometimes, simply the threat of a strike may induce concessions from the opponents.

Strikes may be conducted by agricultural workers and peasants, industrial and office workers, or other groups. Strikes may be full withdrawals of labor, or be restricted in some way, as in a slow-down. They may take many forms, including protest strikes, quickie walkouts, peasant strikes, farm workers' strikes, prisoners' strikes, professional strikes, industry strikes, working-to-rule strikes, reporting "sick," and general strikes. Business owners and workers may unite in producing an economic shutdown.

Strikes may be symbolic to express views. For example, on January 15, 1923, four days after the Franco-Belgian invasion of the Ruhr, the population of the Ruhr and the Rhineland held a thirty-minute protest strike to express its will to resist. Beginning only hours after the entry of Russian troops into Prague in August 1968, the Czechs conducted a number of protest strikes to signal their intention to defy the invaders. On November, 27, 1989, millions of Czechs and Slovaks brought their country to a standstill in a two-hour general strike to show support for free elections and opposition to Communist domination.

Much more often strikes are intended to wield economic power. There is a long history in many countries of the use of strikes by trade unions to improve wages and working conditions. On occasion, however, strikes are directed to achieve political or revolutionary objectives. From April 29 to May 8, 1943, a wave of strikes occurred in the Nazi-occupied Netherlands, involving a majority of industrial workers protesting the planned internment of Dutch army veterans in Germany. Beginning June 30, 1944, Danish workers held a five-day general strike to force the Germans to withdraw the state of martial law and to remove the hated Danish fascist *Schalburgkorps* from Denmark. Negotiations produced some German concessions.

Labor strikes may be combined with business closures to produce economic shutdowns. Such action was a key factor in the struggle to restore Finnish autonomy within Imperial Russia in late 1905. A fully nonviolent business shutdown in 1956 was also a key factor in the ouster of Haitian strongman General Magliore from the presidency.

Political noncooperation involves refusal to continue the usual forms of political participation under existing conditions. Individuals and small groups may practice such methods. However, political noncooperation usually involves larger numbers of people, government personnel, or even governments themselves.

Political noncooperation may take an almost infinite variety of expressions, depending upon the particular situation. Basically, they all stem from a desire not to assist the opponents by performing certain types of political behavior. Political noncooperation may take the form of rejection of the ruler's legitimacy and authority; boycott of governmental bodies and edicts; noncooperation and disobedience of diverse types; stalling and noncooperation by government officers, employees, and constituent units; and international governmental action. Civil disobedience—the deliberate, open, peaceful violation of particular laws, decrees, regulations, ordinances, military or police orders—is one of the best known of these methods.

The purpose of political noncooperation may simply be protest or personal dissociation. More frequently, however, an act of political noncooperation is designed to exert pressure on the government, on an illegitimate group attempting to seize control of the governmental apparatus, or sometimes on another government. The aim of political noncooperation may be to achieve a limited objective, to change the government's policies, to alter its composition, or even to destroy it. Practiced against internal usurpers, a puppet government, or a foreign occupier's administration, the aim of political noncooperation may be to defeat the attack and to restore the legitimate government.

Various types of political noncooperation were significant factors of resistance in all four cases cited in Chapter One. Political noncooperation is the key component of denying legitimacy to the usurpers or occupiers. If granted, legitimacy leads to the more ready availability of such other important sources of power as human assistance, administration, economic resources, and the like. On January 19, 1923, the German government forbade all state and local authorities to obey any Franco-Belgian occupation orders, instructing them to comply only with pre-invasion German authorities. In Czechoslovakia, in 1968, three days after the Soviet invasion, the lord mayor of Prague refused even to see representatives of the occupation forces that had been sent to negotiate with him.

Among the many forms of political noncooperation is the boycott of government-supported organizations, such as the refusal of Norwegian teachers to become members of the new fascist-controlled teachers association created by the Quisling regime in 1942. The refusal to assist troops or police, to acknowledge appointed "officials," or to dissolve existing institutions are also important in this regard. General administrative noncooperation was a key factor in the defeat of the Kapp *Putsch*. In occupied Norway both Norwegian police and German soldiers were sometimes deliberately inefficient in making arrests and even facilitated escapes. Large-scale mutinies of Imperial Russian troops were an important factor in the February 1917 Revolution, which ousted the tsar.

The capacity of the nonviolent resisters to wield the weapons of noncooperation—social, economic, or political—is of extreme importance in the dynamics of a particular nonviolent campaign. Such methods may be used both defensively and offensively. Used defensively, these methods may thwart an attack by maintaining independent initiative, behavior patterns, institutions, and the like. Used offensively, noncooperation may attack the operation and even the existence of institutions and organizations that support the attackers.

Nonviolent Intervention

The methods in this final class are distinguished from those in the two above classes by directly interfering in a situation—disrupting it—by nonviolent means. These acts are not intended simply to communicate a viewpoint or to withhold cooperation. Instead, the people using these methods seize the initiative and directly disrupt the system or situation so that it cannot remain as it was unless those intervening are somehow removed or their action neutralized.

The methods in this class may take psychological, physical, social, economic, or political forms. They include fasts, sit-ins, nonviolent obstruction, establishment of new social behavior, stay-in strikes, alternative economic institutions, inviting imprisonment, work-ons without collaboration, and parallel government.

Used offensively, nonviolent intervention may carry the struggle into the opponents' own camp, even without any immediate provocation. These methods may disrupt, and even destroy, established behavior patterns, policies, relationships, or institutions that are seen as objectionable. Or, these methods may establish new, preferred behavior patterns, policies, relationships, or institutions.

Compared with the other classes of nonviolent action, the methods of nonviolent intervention pose a more direct and immediate challenge. However, this does not necessarily mean more rapid success. A first result of the action may be speedier and more severe repression—which, of course, does not necessarily mean defeat. If intervention is successful, however, victory is likely to come more quickly than by noncooperation because the disruptive effects of the intervention are harder to withstand. For example, a sit-in at a lunch counter or an office upsets normal operations more immediately and completely than would, say, picketing or a consumers' boycott to end discrimination.

There are numerous examples of this type of nonviolent action. In the American civil rights campaigns, physical interventions in the forms of sit-ins were used extensively to end racial discrimination at lunch counters. In 1955 a mass nonviolent invasion of Goa took place to defy Portuguese sovereignty over that part of India. In 1953 when Russian tanks were used to disperse a crowd of 25,000 East German protesters, demonstrators sat down and blocked the paths of the tanks. From 1969 to 1971, Native Americans nonviolently occupied Alcatraz Island in the hope of reclaiming it as unused tribal land. During the German occupation of their country, Poles established an alternative, independent educational system outside of Nazi control. In Czechoslovakia in August and September 1968 an alternative radio broadcast system operated for a full two weeks, defying the Soviet invaders, refuting their propaganda, offering information about events and individuals, and giving instructions for further nonviolent resistance. On December 11, 1989, tens of thousands of protesters encircled the state security headquarters building in Leipzig, East Germany, forcing the head of the local security forces to concede to a filmed "people's inspection" of the security complex. Thirty "inspectors" documented evidence of state "spying" on Leipzig citizens and halted the destruction of incriminating documents.

Parallel government can be an especially important factor in nonviolent struggles in which the whole direction of the society and political system is at stake, as in revolutionary situations or national defense against internal usurpations or foreign occupations. In a revolutionary situation, parallel government refers to the establishment of a new sovereignty that aims to replace the existing one. A new political structure evolves to claim the support and allegiance of the populace. A parallel government emerges and with widespread popular support gradually takes over the governmental functions, eventually squeezing the old regime out of existence by delegitimation and disuse.

This method of nonviolent struggle has hitherto lacked careful analysis and comparative study. The phenomenon has occurred in diverse situations, sometimes to only a limited extent. However, on occasion, a parallel government has become a significant factor in a struggle, at times even fully replacing the original government.

A classic case is the emergence of parallel governments during the American independence movement in the years 1765–1775. Prior to 1774, colonists resisting Britain's effort to increase its authority over the American colonies innovated many methods of nonviolent struggle. By the time of the crisis of 1774–1775, brought on by the Coercive Acts, Americans had lost confidence that constitutional methods could redress their grievances. In addition, colonial governors in several regions forbade legislatures to remain in session if they were likely to support resistance.

In response, colonists began to form new political institutions and transform existing ones, which included the organizing of provisional legislatures and committees of resistance and governance. This trend was given impetus by the Continental Association, a sophisticated program of economic and political noncooperation adopted by the First Continental Congress in October 1774. An extensive network of local, regional, and colony-wide committees supported and enforced resistance to the Coercive Acts. Along with committees of correspondence established earlier, these committees took on many functions of government. As Ronald McCarthy shows, parallel governing structures performed legislative and executive roles, took responsibility for taxation, and even replaced the courts in some areas. In certain cases, colonial legislatures rejected British sovereignty and became organs of resistance and autonomous governments. In others, entirely new organizations operated as alternative political authorities. At this point, the struggle shifted to a more fundamental level as these bodies became substitute governments.

Very clear examples of parallel government emerged in both the 1905 and 1917 Russian revolutions. In 1905, the Bureau of Zemstvo Congresses exercised considerable authority, and entire regions and nationalities broke off control from the capital and established their own autonomous governments, some of which survived into 1906. Prior to the Bolshevik coup d'état in October 1917, both the Provisional Government and the independent soviets, or councils, exercised governmental powers. Nascent elements of parallel governmental structures also developed in India during the 1930–1931 satyagraha campaign.

In a defensive situation, the role of parallel government can be of extreme importance, as will be discussed in Chapter Four.

Wielding Power

To a degree that has never been adequately appreciated, the nonviolent technique operates by changing power relationships. Nonviolent action wields power, both to counter the power of an opponent group and to advance the objectives of the nonviolent group.

This technique of conflict wields power in ways that diverge significantly from popular assumptions about conflict and struggle—in particular, the assumption that violence can be effectively met only with violence. Nonviolent methods are much more complex than previously thought, and are clearly more diverse and complicated than comparable processes of political violence. This is, at least in part, because nonviolent struggle is able to strike at the bases of the opponents' system.

No two cases of nonviolent action are ever exactly alike. They will differ in many respects, including the influences and pressures wielded by the nonviolent group, the responses of the opponents, and the nature of the conflict situation. Nevertheless, it is possible to indicate significant characteristics that are likely to be present in the operation of these conflicts.

Several interrelated forces and processes are likely to operate simultaneously during a given nonviolent campaign. In most cases these will include the effects of the significant increase, or even multiplication of, noncooperating and defiant subjects, the persistence of the resisters in the face of repression, and possible pressures by third parties. Psychological and morale factors, which are highly important in conventional military campaigns and guerrilla warfare, are of still greater importance in nonviolent struggles.

The nonviolent technique can be viewed both as striking at the opponents' power more *directly* and also more *indirectly* than does violence. Violence in its various forms operates primarily by efforts to wound and kill members of the opponents' military forces and, at times, various officials and aides. This is often accompanied by large-scale physical destruction. The military forces and the capacity to conduct military campaigns are themselves the products of the political, social, and economic power of the regime and depend upon much deeper sources of power than, say, quantities of tanks, rifles, or bombs. Military efforts to counter the opponents' military power can therefore be viewed as attacking *expressions* of the opponents' power rather than removing its bases.

In contrast, the nonviolent technique strikes at the very sources of the opponents' power, thus operating more *directly* than does political violence. Each of the sources of the opponents' power, identified in the previous chapter, depends directly or indirectly on the obedience and cooperation of their own agents and officials, the general population, and the institutions of the society. Noncooperation and defiance subvert the needed obedience and cooperation. For example, rejection of the rulers' legitimacy reduces a crucial reason for obedience by both aides and the general populace; extensive popular disobedience and defiance creates immense enforcement problems; massive strikes can paralyze the economy; widespread administrative noncooperation of the bureaucracy can thwart governmental operations; and mutinies of the opponents' police and troops can dissolve the opponents' capacity to repress nonviolent resisters.

Nonviolent struggle operates directly against the opponents in another way. It can be focused on the issue at stake, rather than at military forces or pieces of geography that are often only tangentially related to the conflict. For example, if the crux of the conflict is primarily economic, then economic action, such as boycotts or strikes, may be appropriate. In response to excessive working hours, for example, workers can simply go home at the end of a certain time, as they did in seeking the eight-hour day during the Russian 1905 Revolution. The struggle would then largely hinge on the opponents' vulnerability to those economic leverages and the workers' capacity to withhold economic cooperation. Similarly, if the issues are primarily political, then political action may be most effective. For example, when the Kappists attempted to seize control from the Weimar Republic, the civil servants, bureaucrats, and governments of the states simply refused to acknowledge their legitimacy or to do their bidding in any way. That was fatal for the coup.

More specifically, if censorship of the press and publishing is an issue, then defiance of censorship regulations can be applied to nullify them. Publications can be issued in complete disregard of established laws either openly, in appropriate circumstances, or clandestinely. Such means were used widely in the Russian 1905 Revolution, the Dutch resistance to the Nazi occupation, the Polish struggle of 1980–1989 for greater freedom, and the Palestinian resistance to Israeli occupation. During the Nazi-occupation of Denmark, 538 illegal newspapers were published. In 1944 their combined circulation was over ten million.

The nonviolent technique may also be viewed as striking at the opponents' power more *indirectly* than does violence. Instead of confronting the opponents' police, troops, and the like with forces of the same type, the nonviolent resisters confront them indirectly without counterviolence. This operates to undermine the opponents while helping to mobilize increased strength and support for the cause that the resisters espouse.

For example, by responding to repression nonviolently instead of with counterviolence, those using nonviolent action may demonstrate that the opponents' repression is incapable of both intimidating the populace into submission and provoking resisters into using the very methods that the opponents are well equipped to counteract. This continued resistance while maintaining nonviolent discipline may have other advantages for the resisters. The contrast of violent repression against nonviolent resisters may alienate the opponents' usual supporters, hence weakening their relative power position. The number of nonviolent fighters may grow and support for them may also increase significantly. All this may happen because the opponents' violence is countered indirectly instead of violently. This is the process of "political jiujitsu," which is discussed later in this chapter.

In this type of conflict situation, both the relative power and the absolute power of each of the contending groups are subject to constant and, at times, rapid and extreme changes. This is because the degrees of support given to each may vary considerably and continuously, increasing or decreasing the availability of the crucial sources of power. These variations in power can be much greater and can occur more quickly than in situations where both sides use violence. In this asymmetrical conflict situation, nonviolent struggle is directly altering the very sources of the power of each side. The impact of this is felt more immediately than in a strictly violent conflict, which affects those sources only indirectly.

The nonviolent strategists must capitalize on these potential sudden changes in each side's power. To do this, the practitioners of nonviolent struggle must seek to influence the strengths and loyalties of three groups. First, they need to seek continually to increase their own strength and that of their supporters. Second, they will also gain strength if they can increase active participation among the wider group affected by the grievances. Third, the nature of nonviolent struggle makes it possible for the resisters to win considerable support even in the opponents' camp and among third parties. This possibility is diminished if violent means are used because the absence of violence enables observers to evaluate the issues at stake independently of reactions to the use of violence. Moreover, reliance on only nonviolent means commonly brings sympathy to the participants in the struggle. The ability to gain support in the opponents' own camp and among third parties gives the nonviolent group a capacity to influence—and at times to regulate indirectly—*its opponents'* power, by reducing or severing its sources.

Usually the results of these complex changes in the relative power positions of the contenders will determine the struggle's final outcome.

The Importance of Strategy

Changes in power relationships will be greatly influenced, and the whole course of the struggle to a large degree shaped, by the strategy and tactics applied and the specific methods used by the nonviolent group. Strategy is just as important in nonviolent action as in military warfare.

The aim of a strategy is to use one's resources to maximum advantage to gain one's objectives at minimum cost. The specific methods of nonviolent action used will be most effective if they work together to implement an overall strategy or conception of how to accomplish the objectives. The strategy and tactics chosen and the methods used will help to determine which power sources will be affected and the degree to which they are reduced or severed. These should normally be related to specific issues. Usually, for example, economic action is appropriate for economic issues, and political noncooperation and intervention for political issues. There is far from a universal pattern, however, and at times economic resistance can be very useful in a struggle whose issues are primarily political. In all cases, the action needs to be finely tuned as part of a carefully developed overall plan.

The nonviolent strategists need, therefore, to plan their strategy with much thought and extreme care, drawing upon the best available resources about strategic principles and their own knowledge of nonviolent struggle and the conflict situation. General discussions of strategy in nonviolent struggle are available elsewhere, and some of the strategic principles and options in civilian-based defense will be discussed in Chapter Four.

The Importance of the Loci of Power

The ability to conduct nonviolent struggle will be highly influenced by the independent institutions and groupings in the society that may conduct and support such action, as discussed in Chapter Two. That discussion showed that nonviolent struggle will be greatly strengthened when it is conducted by, or with the support of, the established institutions of the society such as professional organizations, religious institutions, trade unions, political parties, and social organizations, and has the backing of regional, cultural, national, or kinship groupings, and even local, provincial, and regional governments or their subdivisions.

Loci of power may also be less formally organized, or may be created just prior to or during the nonviolent struggle. Or, they may be older bodies that had been long inactive or that had their capacity for independent action and initiative weakened drastically by deliberate measures of a highly centralized political system. Such bodies may become revitalized in the process of achieving some objective or of broadly opposing the rulers or attackers of their society. Therefore, both newly created loci and revitalized ones are likely to play significant roles in the conduct of nonviolent struggle.

This was the case, as noted above, in the nonviolent phase of the American independence movement with the formation of the committees of correspondence and the extralegal provincial governments in 1774 and 1775. In Rhode Island, for example, established local governments, town meetings, and even the official provincial government became key instruments against British rule in the three noncooperation campaigns of 1765–1775.

During the nonviolent first phase of the 1956 Hungarian Revolution, a new, vast, and powerful workers' council movement developed among factory workers, professionals, and other groups. The movement quickly took on political dimensions, federating to form for some weeks a substitute national government, until, in the violent second phase of the revolution, the Russians defeated the Hungarian army.

In various other cases, long-established organizations have served similar roles as bases of resistance, such as sports clubs, teachers' organizations, and, in Norway during the Nazi occupation, the State Church. In resistance to the Kapp Putsch, political parties, trade unions, provincial governments and other bodies were crucial. In the Czechoslovak resistance of 1968 even the Communist Party became for some weeks an instrument of resistance against the Russians. In the Polish movement for democratization in the 1980s the independent trade union Solidarity and a variety of other newly created organizations, including students' and peasants' groups, became powerful bodies in the struggle. (Despite martial law after a military coup d'état, these bodies, while weakened, were not eradicated.) These and other loci, such as underground publishing houses, were instrumental in the continuation and strengthening of the democratic forces in Poland in the late 1980s.

The Opponents' Problems

The challenge presented by nonviolent action may be a mild one and disturb the status quo only slightly. In extreme cases, however, the challenge may shatter it. In any event, attention will have been called to the grievances and to the presence of the opposition. The underlying conflict will be brought into the open, probably leading to an initial polarizing of opinion.

Opponents facing strong nonviolent action may be seriously threatened. The gravity of this challenge will vary with such factors as the issues of grievances at stake and their apparent justification; the quality of the action; the numbers participating; how the withdrawal of obedience and cooperation is expressed; and the ability of the resisters to maintain their nonviolent discipline and their refusal to submit despite the opponents' reprisals. The outcome will also, in part, be determined by the social and political milieu in which the struggle takes place. These basic conditions include the degree of nonconformity the system can tolerate without altering its nature; the degree of support for, or hostility to, the regime among all groups involved; the chances that noncooperation and defiance will spread; and, finally, the degree to which the material, human, moral, and institutional sources of power necessary for the government's existence continue to be available, are restricted, or are withdrawn.

The opponents' difficulties in coping with nonviolent action are consequences of the special dynamics and mechanisms of the technique (which will be examined shortly). These difficulties do not depend on their being surprised by the absence of violence or being unfamiliar with the technique. The opponents' knowledge of nonviolent struggle, for example, does not by itself provide the capacity to defeat the nonviolent fighters. In wars, both sides use their knowledge of military struggle to increase their chances of success. In nonviolent struggles, with more knowledge, the opponents may become more sophisticated in countermeasures, and perhaps less cruel and more able to face the issues. However, the nonviolent group also may learn how to struggle more skillfully and how to respond to the opponents' controls and sophistication more effectively.

Only very rarely, if ever, do governments and other hierarchical systems face the extremes of having complete support or none. Most frequently they receive partial support. Even when the regime is eventually destroyed by disobedience, noncooperation, and defiance, it may have been supported sufficiently and long enough to inflict brutal repression against the nonviolent group. It is therefore necessary to explore how the nonviolent technique operates in struggle against violent opponents, the several ways in which changes are finally produced, and the specific factors that determine whether a given campaign will be a success, a failure, or something in between.

It is an error to equate using nonviolent struggle with keeping the opponents good-natured. The opponents are not likely to appreciate a challenge to their power or policies, even if the challenge is nonviolent. If the action poses a serious threat to their control, and if they do not intend to grant the resisters' demands, the opponents must react.

Repression

Nonviolent action is designed to operate against opponents who are able and willing to use violent sanctions. In fact, nonviolent struggle has been employed against such violent regimes as Nazi Germany, the Communist governments in Poland, East Germany, Hungary, Bulgaria, Rumania, China, Yugoslavia, and the Soviet Union, Jorge Ubico's Guatemala, El Salvador under Maximiliano Hernández Martínez, Pinochet's Chile, apartheid South Africa, and Burma under Ne Win. Such opponents, when faced with the nonviolent challenge, are most unlikely suddenly to renounce their violence, or even to restrict it consistently.

Repression is therefore a likely response to a serious nonviolent challenge. Repression can take such forms as censorship, confiscation of funds and property, severance of communications, economic pressure, arrests, imprisonments, conscription, concentration camps, use of *agents provocateurs*, threats, beatings, shootings, massacres, torture, martial law, executions, and retaliation against relatives and friends. The amount and type of repression will vary, being influenced by several factors. The repression of the nonviolent group, however, may be significantly more limited than the opponents would use against a violent rebellion or a foreign enemy using military means. This is not because of any gentility, but derives from a recognition that extreme violent repression can be counterproductive to the regime that is facing the nonviolent challenge.

The high probability of violent repression is strong evidence that nonviolent action can pose a real threat to the established order. This is a confirmation of, and tribute to, the power of the technique. The opponents' violence is no more a reason for abandoning nonviolent action than is the enemy's military action in a war a reason to abandon one's own military action.

The violence of such repression may also be in part a demonstration of the underlying nature of that system. This demonstration may influence the course of the struggle. Extreme repression may vividly expose the violent nature of the system to many citizens and third parties, possibly further alienating support for the opponents and increasing assistance to the nonviolent resisters.

As was pointed out in the previous chapter, repression will not necessarily produce submission. For the opponents' sanctions to be effective, they must operate on the minds of the subjects, producing fear and the willingness to obey. Just as in war, however, there is the likelihood that planning and discipline, or some overriding loyalty or objective, will cause the nonviolent fighters to persist despite the dangers.

In case after case, contrary to what might be expected, there has been independent testimony that people have not submitted to such fear. They have either, as in the front lines of war, learned to control their fear or, more dramatically, have apparently lost their fear. The action of the women of the Plaza del Mayo in Buenos Aires who persistently paraded with the photographs of their "disappeared" husbands or children is only one small example of this defiance in face of danger. Gerald Reitlinger—an early scholar of the Holocaust—gave a large part of the credit for the saving of more than 75 percent of the Jews in France from extermination to the refusal of French people to submit and comply in the face of Gestapo terror and other intimidation: "the final solution . . . failed in France because of the sense of decency in the common man, who, having suffered the utmost depths of self-humiliation, learnt to conquer fear." When officials conducted mass arrests and private persons resorted to bombings during the Montgomery, Alabama, bus boycott, the result was increased determination and fearlessness by the city's African-Americans. Martin Luther King, Jr., wrote that "The members of the opposition . . . were not aware they were dealing with Negroes who had been freed from fear. And so every move they made proved to be a mistake." In Halle, East Germany, on June 17, 1953, although Russian tanks had been patrolling the city streets and the People's Police had been firing warning shots into the air, between 60,000 and 80,000 people attended a mass anti-government meeting in the city market place. In Manila in February 1986 masses of peaceful Filipinos blocked the paths of army tanks sent to attack disobedient military officers and troops.

Combative Nonviolent Discipline

Faced with violent repression, nonviolent resisters, if they have the strength, must persist and refuse to submit or retreat. They must be willing to risk punishment as a part of the price of victory. The chances and severity of repression will vary. This risk is not unique to nonviolent action, however. There are also risks—usually far more severe—when both sides use violence.

Nonviolent discipline refers especially to the maintenance of persistent nonviolent behavior even in the face of violent repression. However, in planned campaigns, nonviolent discipline also includes orderly adherence to the predetermined strategy, tactics, methods of action, and the like.

There are in history many examples of groups defying overwhelming violence, both violently and nonviolently, while pursuing the struggle with impressive discipline. Among these examples are the brave defense by Spartan soldiers who fought to the last man against the vastly superior Persian army at Thermopylae in 480 B.C. and the 1944 uprising against the Nazis by the Jews of the Warsaw ghetto. In a myriad of cases, nonviolent combatants, too, have overcome fear of reprisals, or even death, and continued their disciplined defiance. These examples range from Indian nationalists who in 1930 refused to retreat from their raid on a salt depot at Dharasana in the face of British-ordered beatings that fractured skulls, to the Berlin women who returned to their protest seeking their Jewish husbands' release despite the threat of being machine-gunned.

The nonviolent group in a repressive situation must maintain nonviolent discipline to gain increased control over their opponents, to reduce the violence against themselves, and to increase their chances of winning. Maintaining nonviolent discipline in the face of repression is not an act of moralistic naiveté. Instead, it is a requirement for success and is a prerequisite for advantageous shifts in power relationships. Nonviolent discipline can be compromised only at the severe risk of contributing to defeat. Other factors are, of course, highly important too, and maintaining nonviolent discipline alone will not ensure victory.

Faced with repression and suffering, the nonviolent group will need to make efforts to strengthen its morale, feelings of solidarity, and determination to continue the struggle. Advance training in the use of nonviolent action and how to behave under stress can help in these efforts. People may also become more disciplined as they learn from direct experience that the rigorous application of the nonviolent technique bears great advantages for them. The nonviolent fighters may also learn from their own experience (and that of others) that their nonviolent response to violence may reduce casualties. While resisters and bystanders do get wounded and killed during nonviolent struggle, the numbers are consistently much smaller than in comparable violent resistance movements, such as violent insurrections, guerrilla warfare, and conventional military wars. An awareness of all these factors may help people to maintain the required discipline during harsh repression.

Opponents may wish the resisters had instead chosen violent means, which do not present the same kind of enforcement problems. Since the opponents are generally better equipped to deal with violence, they may therefore deliberately seek to provoke the resisters into violence, either by severe repression or by the use of spies and *agents provocateurs*. For example, in combating the Finnish nonviolent noncooperation movement for independence from tsarist Russia in the first years of the twentieth century, the Russian governor-general arranged for the Ochrana (the Russian secret police) to hire *agents provocateurs* to commit violence against Russians or to instigate such violence by Finns to help justify savage repression of the movement.

If the nonviolent group maintains its discipline, persists despite repression and other control measures, and conducts massive noncooperation and defiance involving significant sectors of the populace, the result may be that the opponents' will is effectively blocked.

The arrest of leaders may simply lead to the movement developing in such a way that it can carry on without a recognizable leadership. The opponents may make new acts illegal, only to find that attempts to repress defiance at certain points are countered by a broadened nonviolent attack on other fronts. The opponents may find that massive repression, instead of forcing cooperation and obedience, is constantly met by refusal to submit or to flee. Not only may repression prove inadequate to control defiant subjects, but agencies of repression may, in extreme cases, also be immobilized by the massive defiance. There may be just too many people defying the system in too many places to be controlled by the available police and troops.

While the suffering can be severe, there is no more reason for alarm in the face of the opponents' anger and repression than there is for military officers to panic at the first sign of casualties. The comparable situation in a nonviolent struggle, however, must be handled wisely. If it appears that the opponents are simply becoming brutalized, or that resisters are not able to withstand the suffering, a change in tactics and methods may be required within the framework of nonviolent struggle. Barring that, however, there is reason to believe that the brutalities are a temporary phase, though not necessarily a brief one. Brutality thrives on fear, anger, or counterviolence. In their absence and where there is evidence that both the repression and the brutality react upon and weaken the opponents' own position, the opponents will tend to reduce their violence.

Political Jiujitsu

Repression of a nonviolent group that both persists in struggle and also maintains nonviolent discipline triggers the special process of "political jiujitsu." This process throws the opponents off balance politically because their violent thrusts are met with neither violent resistance nor with surrender.

Brutality against a nonviolent group is more difficult to justify (to the opponents' own people or to the world at large) than brutality against violent rebels. The degree to which a regime will feel able to defy world—or domestic—opinion will of course vary, but a problem remains. News of brutalities may eventually leak out despite censorship, and harsher repression may increase rather than reduce hostility and resistance to the regime.

The opponents' repression, when confronted with the discipline, solidarity, and persistence of the nonviolent challengers, puts the opponents in the worst possible light. As cruelties to nonviolent people increase, the opponents' regime may appear still more despicable, and sympathy and support for the nonviolent side may grow still more from several quarters. The general population may become more alienated from the opponents' regime and more willing to join the resistance, so that the numbers of the resisting population increase and they become more determined to continue despite the costs. Persons divorced from the immediate conflict may increase support for the victims of the repression and turn against both the brutalities and the policies of the repressing regime. On November 17, 1989, Czech riot police brutally suppressed nonviolent demonstrators demanding free elections and democracy in the streets of Prague. These beatings galvanized political opposition to the hard-line Communist regime. Czechs and Slovaks erected shrines at the main sites of the beatings, raising those injured to the stature of heroes. Hundreds of thousands took to the streets daily following the police actions. As one student put it, the beatings were "the spark that started the whole movement." Within four weeks the Communist hard-liners were forced to resign, and the Communist Party had to relinquish its majority of Cabinet positions.

The effect of national and international public opinion varies widely, and cannot be relied upon to effect major change. Nevertheless, such opinion may play an important role. It may rally to the support of the nonviolent challengers and may at times lead to significant political and economic pressures against the opponents' regime.

Finally, even the opponents' own supporters, agents, and troops may become disturbed by the brutalities committed against nonviolent people and may begin to doubt the justice of their government's policies as well as the morality of the repression. Their initial uneasiness may grow into dissent and at times even into noncooperation and disobedience, perhaps leading to strikes and mutinies.

Thus, if repression leads to an increase in the number of nonviolent fighters and enlarges defiance, and if it leads to sufficient opposition among the supporters of the opponents so that their capacity to deal with the defiance and continue their policies is reduced, the repression will clearly have rebounded against the opponents. This is "political jiujitsu" at work.

Significant elements of political jiujitsu have occurred in a great variety of cases. The massacre of hundreds of nonviolent petitioners near the Winter Palace in St. Petersburg in January 1905 turned hitherto loyal masses into defiant revolutionaries, launching a year-long revolution throughout the Russian Empire. The killings of hundreds of nonviolent demonstrators by Russian troops in February 1917 was a major factor in producing widespread mutinies and desertions of the tsar's soldiers, making it impossible to save the imperial system from the predominantly nonviolent February Revolution. Severe repression in the Ruhr in 1923 not only aroused international support for the Germans but opposition to the policy in France itself. The brutality of British repression of nonviolent nationalists in India, in the 1920s and 1930s especially, aroused much opposition in Britain and added to the growth of support for Indian independence. The Sharpeville massacre in South Africa in 1960 aroused massive international protests, boycotts, and embargoes. The brutal repression in 1963 of nonviolent Buddhists opposing the Ngo Dinh Diem regime caused the United States to withdraw its support from the government to which it had been committed for years. Beatings, killings, bombings, and the like against civil rights demonstrators in the United States in the 1950s and 1960s, as in Montgomery, Atlanta, Birmingham, and various places in Mississippi, rebounded to increase protests and gain widespread American and in-

ternational support for an end to both the repression and the segregation policies. The massacre of hundreds, if not thousands, of Chinese in
Tiananman Square, other parts of Beijing, and elsewhere in China on
June 4, 1989 (and the following days), further undermined the authority of the Communist regime and aroused deep opposition to it in
China and throughout the world. The full consequences of this massacre await to be seen.

Four Mechanisms of Change

Despite the variations among cases of nonviolent action, it is possible
to distinguish four general "mechanisms" of change that operate in
nonviolent action. These are *conversion, accommodation, nonviolent coercion,* and *disintegration.*

Conversion

In conversion, the opponents, as a result of the actions of the nonviolent group, adopt a new point of view and accept the goals of that
group. Such change may be brought about by reason and argumenta-
tion, though it is doubtful that such intellectual efforts alone will produce conversion. Conversion in nonviolent action is likely also to involve the opponents' emotions, beliefs, attitudes, and moral system.
The nonviolent group may deliberately seek conversion so that in the
end the opponents not only *grant* the objectives of the nonviolent group
but also *want* to grant them, feeling that it is right to do so.

In conversion attempts, the suffering of the nonviolent combatants
may play a major role in affecting the opponents' emotions. Conversion will often be difficult, in part because barriers to clear perception
may exist. These include the phenomenon of "social distance"—a failure to recognize members of another social group as fellow human
beings who merit empathy and respect. It may therefore take a considerable period of time to eliminate social distance and achieve conversion, if it ever does happen.

One case where it did occur took place in Vykom, South India, in
1924–1925. Gandhi's supporters sought to gain the right of the "untouchables" to use a road passing an orthodox Brahman temple. A
group of high-caste Hindu reformers together with their untouchable
friends first attempted simply to walk down the road, stopping in front
of the temple. Orthodox Hindus attacked the protesters severely, and
the maharajah's police arrested some of them, who received prison sen-

tences of up to a year. Volunteers arrived from all over India and a continuous vigil was held in the road at the police barricade. Volunteers, operating in shifts, stood in an attitude of prayer through the hot sunny months and the rainy season, sometimes with water to their shoulders while the police patrolled in boats. When the maharajah's government finally removed the barricade, the demonstrators declined to walk forward until the orthodox Hindus changed their minds. Finally, after sixteen months, the local Brahmans said: "We cannot any longer resist the prayers that have been made to us, and we are ready to receive the untouchables." The case had wide reverberations throughout India.

The Vykom vigil is far from typical of nonviolent action, however. For a variety of reasons, efforts to convert opponents by nonviolent suffering may be ineffective. Also, some nonviolent strategists may reject conversion as undesirable, unnecessary, or impossible. Hence they may seek change by the other mechanisms of accommodation, nonviolent coercion, or even disintegration. In most situations, the outcomes are likely to result from the combined pressure of elements of all four mechanisms, no one of which being fully carried to culmination. The most successful applications of nonviolent action may involve the wise and deliberate combination of these elements. For example, efforts to convert some members of the opponents' population can assist accommodation and successful efforts to convert the opponents' soldiers can lead to nonviolent coercion.

Accommodation

Accommodation is an intermediary mechanism between conversion and nonviolent coercion. The opponents are neither converted nor nonviolently coerced; yet elements of both mechanisms are involved in the opponents' decision to grant concessions to the nonviolent group. This is probably the most common mechanism of the four in successful nonviolent campaigns. Here, the opponents grant all or some demands without fundamentally changing their minds about the issues.

In contrast to conversion, the mechanism of accommodation (as well as nonviolent coercion and disintegration) brings success by *changing the social, economic, or political situation* by nonviolent action, rather than changing the minds and hearts of the opponents' leadership. Basic power relationships have changed so as to alter the entire picture.

Accommodation occurs, however, while the opponents are still able to *choose* whether to grant concessions. The opponents may agree to accommodate in order to undercut internal dissension and actual opposition within their own group. In economic struggles, accommodation may result from an effort to minimize losses, especially from strikes and economic boycotts. The opponents may also decide to accommodate voluntarily to the demands if they anticipate that the nonviolent movement will grow in strength. The specific issues at stake may be of less importance than the possible consequences of a protracted struggle, which may include the populace discovering its considerable power. Such consequences may have long-term effects on the social structure and political processes of the society. A face-saving formula may be important in a settlement resulting from accommodation, with the opponents not wanting to appear that they have capitulated to the resistance.

The mechanism of accommodation operates in the settlement of many cases when nonviolent action is used. It is most obvious in the settlement of labor strikes, in which (as is almost always the case) the final settlement of issues lies somewhere between the original positions of the employers and the trade union. In larger international conflicts, accommodation is also sometimes involved. Indian independence from Britain in 1947 did not occur directly as a consequence of a particular nonviolent campaign, but highly significant elements of accommodation were involved, derived in part from the struggles of the previous decades. Accommodation resulted from the recognition that independence for India was a legitimate policy, that it would be exceptionally difficult if not impossible even with British military force to keep India under British control, and that economic gains to Britain from India had disappeared in part because of the boycott movements and the high cost of maintaining administration and repression.

In many situations, neither conversion nor accommodation will be achieved, for some opponents will remain unwilling to grant any of the demands of the nonviolent resisters. A third mechanism of change then remains open to the challengers: nonviolent coercion, which can lead to success contrary to the will of the opponents.

Coercion

"Coercion" needs to be understood here with a more precise meaning than is frequently the case. Coercion does not here mean submitting under threat or use of superior force. Instead, "coercion" here is the forcing or blocking of change against the opponents' will. The opponents' ability to act effectively has been taken away from them, but they still retain sufficient power to hold their positions and to capitulate to the resisters' demands. In short, "nonviolent coercion" as a mechanism of nonviolent action occurs when goals are achieved against the will of the opponents, but short of the disintegration of the opponents' system.

Nonviolent action becomes coercive when the nonviolent resisters succeed directly or indirectly in withholding to a major degree the necessary sources of the opponents' political power: authority, human resources, skills and knowledge, intangible factors, material resources, and sanctions.

Nonviolent coercion may be produced when the opponents' will is blocked in any of three ways. First, the defiance may become too widespread and massive to be controlled by repressive measures. Changes in the status quo may be made—or blocked—by the mass action, so that the opponents' agreement or acquiescence is irrelevant. Second, the system may be paralyzed by the resistance. Noncooperation may make it impossible for the social, economic, and political systems to continue to operate unless the resisters' demands are met and the noncooperators resume their normal duties. Third, even the opponents' ability to apply repression may be undermined and at times dissolved. This occurs when their soldiers and police mutiny, their bureaucracy refuses to provide assistance, or their populace withdraws authority and support. In any of these circumstances, or in any combination of them, the opponents may find that they are unable to defend their policies or system in the face of determined and widespread nonviolent action, even though their aims remain unchanged. This frustration of the opponents' efforts is usually directly proportionate to the extent of the noncooperation and defiance.

Blockage of the opponents' will appears to result more frequently from massive resistance and paralysis of the system than from the dissolution of the opponents' ability to apply repression. That pattern may, however, be reversed in certain circumstances. In nonviolent coercion, nonviolent action has so altered the social and political situation that the opponents can no longer wield power in ways contrary to the will of the nonviolent group.

In some very successful labor strikes, the employers have simply given in to virtually all the demands of the unions (including, in past decades, recognition of those organizations as bargaining agents) because the employers no longer had an effective choice. Tsar Nicholas II of Imperial Russia, completely against his beliefs, issued the constitutional manifesto of October 17, 1905, granting a duma (parliament). He seems to have had no choice, although he remained tsar. The 1905 Great October Strike in Russia was so effective and inclusive that for a while the government was simply unable to govern and the country was gripped by what was called "some strange paralysis." The departure from the presidency of both General Hernández Martínez of El

Salvador and General Ubico of Guatemala in the spring of 1944 in the face of massive economic shutdowns and political noncooperation were cases of coercion. The departures occurred even before their administrative, police, and military systems collapsed around them.

Disintegration

When the sources of power are nearly completely withheld from the opponents, they will not simply be coerced. Their system of government may in fact be dissolved. This mechanism of nonviolent change operates by removing the sources of power to a sufficiently extreme degree that the opponents' system of government simply falls apart. Only individuals or very small, largely powerless, groups remain. Coercion does not take place because there is no longer any effective unit to be coerced. The populace has overwhelmingly repudiated the authority of the opponents either to rule or to provide any leadership, guidance, or control. Virtually no one will any longer assist the former dominant group. Hence, those individuals and groups that once were powerful no longer possess the expertise and economic resources that enabled them to function in the past. In addition, the police and military forces have either mutinied against their former masters or have simply fallen apart so that no organized system of repression remains. The mechanism of disintegration is the most extreme application of withdrawal of the sources of power.

As a result of the massive noncooperation in the February 1917 Revolution in Imperial Russia, Tsar Nicholas II abdicated, but his military commander in Petrograd did not know to whom to surrender. George Katkov concluded that the Imperial government had just been "dissolved and swept away." In the 1920 Kapp Putsch and the Algiers generals' coup in 1961, it is clear that as a result of the withholding and withdrawal of needed support, both of those attempted usurpations simply disintegrated.

When disintegration of the opponents' regime occurs in the absence of an alternative legitimate government, other governmental institutions will develop. Sometimes a parallel government (discussed earlier in this chapter) emerges. If it has already done so, or if the legitimate government has survived in some form from the past, as before a coup d'état or invasion, it can, at the point of the opponents' disintegration, expand its authority and influence and consolidate its power. This is a time for vigilance by the resisters, as unrepresentative military or political groups may attempt to seize control of the state apparatus in order to establish a new dictatorship, rather than allowing the development or restoration of a popularly based democratic system.

Factors Influencing Coercion and Disintegration

A variety of factors may produce nonviolent coercion or disintegration. The sources of power affected will vary, as will the degree to which they are severed. Variations, therefore, exist in the pattern of action that produces the nonviolent coercion or disintegration: massive defiance, economic or political paralysis, or mutiny. Some or all of the following factors will determine the outcome:

> the number of nonviolent resisters and their proportion in the general population;
>
> the degree of the opponents' dependence on the nonviolent resisters for sources of their power;
>
> the skill of the nonviolent resisters in applying the technique, including the choice of strategy, tactics, and methods, and their ability to implement them;
>
> the length of time that the noncooperation and defiance can be maintained;
>
> the degree of sympathy and support for the nonviolent resisters from third parties;
>
> the means of control open to the opponents and used by them to induce consent and force a resumption of cooperation, and the reaction of nonviolent resisters to those means;
>
> the degree to which the opponents' subjects, administrators, and agents support or refuse to support them, and the action that they may undertake to withhold that support and to assist the nonviolent resisters; and
>
> the opponents' estimate of the probable future course of the nonviolent struggle.

Removing the Sources of Power

The specific methods used to remove the sources of power will differ from case to case. Variation also occurs in *who* severs them. It may be the nonviolent group, third parties, disenchanted members of the opponents' own group, or a combination of these factors. These variations make it imperative to carefully analyze strategies that were used in past conflicts or that may be used in the future.

Authority

The nonviolent challenge to opponents clearly demonstrates the degree to which their authority is *already* undermined. The struggle may help to alienate more of the opponents' supporters. At times there will be a clear transfer of loyalty from the opponents to a rival authority, even to a competing parallel government.

The denial of authority to usurpers and aggressors is a key element in preventing the establishment of a new government of oppressors. This was clearly seen in all four of the cases described in Chapter One, but it was most obvious in the defense against the Kapp Putsch and the French generals' coup in Algiers. The persistent refusal to grant the usurpers legitimacy doomed the attacks.

In another example, in February 1943 the Dutch Reformed Church and the Roman Catholic Church in the Netherlands urged their members to commit civil disobedience and to refuse collaboration with Nazi-occupation authorities as religious duties. This action by the Dutch churches reduced the authority of occupation officials and increased the legitimacy of noncooperation and disobedience.

Human resources

Widespread nonviolent action may also reduce or sever the human resources necessary to the opponents' political power, as when the masses of subjects who maintain and operate the system withhold their general obedience and cooperation. Both the economic and the political systems operate because of the contributions of many individuals, organizations, and subgroups. The principle of the general strike can therefore be applied to both the economic and the political system.

In the case of a foreign occupation, two distinct population groups are involved. Although withdrawal of human resources by both the people under occupation and those in the occupier country would be most powerful, the noncooperation of only the people in the occupied country may prove effective given the presence of certain other favorable conditions.

The sheer multiplication of noncooperating, disobedient, and defiant members of the grievance group creates severe enforcement problems for the opponents. Also, the opponents' traditional supporters may at times withdraw their assistance, thereby reducing the opponents' power further.

The withdrawal of human resources will also affect other needed sources of power (skills, knowledge, and material resources). Thus, in a conflict, the opponents will require greater power at the very time that their enforcement capacity is being reduced. If the resistance grows while the opponents' power weakens, eventually the regime may become powerless. This occurred on a relatively small scale among the troops under British command in the Northwest Frontier

Province of British India in April 1930 during the 1930–1931 civil disobedience campaign. In Peshawar, at least 30 and perhaps 125 resisters
were shot to death on April 23, 1930. After this, two platoons of the
Royal Garhwal Rifles, which were ordered to Peshawar, refused to proceed on the ground that their duty did not include shooting "unarmed
brethren." The night of April 24 the British withdrew their troops from
Peshawar, temporarily abandoning the city, which was then controlled
by the local Indian National Congress Committee until British-led rein-
forcements with air support returned on May 4.

Other examples of withdrawal of human resources include the walkout of twenty-nine Philippine computer operators who refused to assist the perpetration of election fraud and the "strike" of major parts of
the Philippine army, which simply refused to carry out repression and
stayed in an army camp, neither initiating civil war nor obeying orders
of the Marcos government.

In Norway during the Nazi occupation in December 1940, the entire Norwegian Supreme Court resigned in protest against the declaration by Reichskommissar Terboven that the Court had no right to
declare his German occupation "laws" unconstitutional. In 1942 the
fascist government of Norwegian "Minister-President" Vidkun Quisling ordered the creation of a dictatorially controlled teachers organization with compulsory membership. It was to be the model for other
"corporations" to be established later, and also an instrument for in-
doctrinating school children. The teachers, however, refused all cooperation with the new organization. Hundreds were arrested and
interned in a concentration camp. Parents protested the government
action and the teachers not arrested refused to be intimidated. Eight
months later the teachers were released. Quisling's desired "Corporative State" never came into existence in Norway, the fascist teachers'
organization was stillborn, and the schools were never used for fascist
propaganda.

Skills and Knowledge

Certain individuals or groups possess special skills or knowledge of
particular importance; they include administrators, officials, technicians, and advisors. Withdrawal of their assistance disproportionately
weakens the rulers' power. Thus, in addition to outright refusal, reduced assistance may also be important.

During the 1923 Kapp Putsch, Dr. Kapp pronounced that a government of experts was needed. However, when qualified men virtually
unanimously refused appointments to his "Cabinet," Kapp was left

without their expertise, having been repudiated by potential competent aides. Officers in the Ministry of War refused to obey orders.
Reichsbank officials refused to allow Kapp to withdraw ten million
marks, citing the lack of an authorized signature. (All of the undersec-
retaries refused to sign and Kapp's own signature was deemed worth-
less.) No notable politicians supported Kapp. The Berlin security police
reversed their initial support and demanded Kapp's resignation, and
numerous other civil servants refused their cooperation. Kapp could
not even find a secretary or a typewriter (all of which were locked in
closets) to have his initial proclamation typed; hence, it did not appear
in the next day's newspapers. This denial of administrative cooperation, combined with a massive general strike, forced the Kappists to
admit defeat and to retreat from Berlin.

Intangible Factors

Habits of obedience and loyalty to authority may also be threatened by
widespread nonviolent action.

The East German Rising of June 16–17, 1953, produced what was to
Communists and their supporters the shocking scene of workers publicly protesting in the streets and denouncing the purported workers'
state. This breaking of the pattern of automatic support and obedience
contributes to further questioning by the rest of the population of
whether or not to obey.

Erosion of faith in Communist ideology and its supposedly noble
goals has been multiplied by the impact of military and government
repression in such places as East Germany, Czechoslovakia, Hungary,
and Poland. Such repression not only led many Communists and their
supporters in those countries to lose their ideological commitment, but
also led to large-scale disaffection by foreign Communist parties, such
as in Italy, and to the resignations of Communist Party members in
various countries.

In other situations, as in Hungary in 1956, massive conformity to the
system that had existed for years was shattered as millions of people
realized that a vast percentage of the population in fact hated the regime. Initial small acts of defiance helped to trigger that awareness and
to launch the first major, nonviolent, phase of the Hungarian Revolution. In 1989 ideological erosion had grown so great—and the people's
willingness to conform had virtually dissolved—in East Germany and
Czechoslovakia that the Communist regimes in each country were
forced to accept fundamental political changes. In Czechoslavakia, the
Communist Party was even forced to hand over the presidency.

Frequently in the course of a nonviolent movement, major spokespersons for accepted moral, religious, and political standards of the society take the lead in denouncing, or support the denunciation of, the oppressive system and urge the population to resist, to change, or to destroy it.

Material Resources

Nonviolent action may reduce or sever the supply of material resources to the opponents. Sixty-one of 198 identified methods of nonviolent action involve economic boycotts or labor strikes, or combinations of them, operating domestically or internationally. They are designed to disrupt, reduce, or destroy the availability of material resources, transportation, raw materials, means of communication, and even, in extreme cases, the capacity of the economic system to function.

Large-scale nonviolent struggles in which the issues were predominantly or avowedly political have often employed economic forms of noncooperation. These have included the noncooperation campaigns of the American colonists against British rule in 1765–1775 and the Indian noncooperation movements against the British in the 1920s and 1930s. Both had enormous economic impact on the British economy and government and induced powerful pressures within Britain in support of the colonials.

While there has been much dispute in recent decades about the effectiveness of international economic sanctions, it is clear that many specific cases of their use have often been ill-conceived and virtually unprepared. However, as the Arab oil embargo of 1973 demonstrated, such sanctions can be very effective in inducing changes in a government's policies (in this particular case, numerous countries altered their foreign policies toward the Middle East).

Within a country, labor strikes for both political and economic objectives have been at times widespread and politically significant. A government whose nature or policies produces strikes that paralyze the economy is unlikely to be very popular or durable. Although not all strikes succeed, they can at times be powerful instruments. The resistance to the Kapp Putsch in March 1920 included what was called "the greatest strike the world had ever seen." This was in spite of the fact that Kapp made picketing a capital offense. The role of strikes in other situations has already been noted.

The Nazis viewed mass noncooperation in the form of a general strike as a most dangerous weapon, especially as they were seeking to consolidate control of the state. After the burning of the *Reichstag* (parliament building) on February 27, 1933—possibly by the Nazis themselves as a provocation to facilitate repression of opponents and thus help gain full state control—the Nazis issued on March 1 a decree that provided punishments both for "provocation to armed conflict against the state" and for "provocation to a general strike." Delarue in his study, *The Gestapo,* writes that at this time "what the Nazis feared the most was a general strike."

Strikes, even general strikes, are not tools to be used routinely on any issue, and especially in defense crises. Their intended impact, the strength of the population to conduct them, and the means for the society to sustain itself during the economic struggle, all have to be carefully considered.

Both strikes and economic boycotts demonstrate the capacity of nonviolent struggle to weaken and remove another of the main sources of power—economic resources—from existing or would-be rulers. With control of the economy, including transportation, communications, and the like, in the hands of a resisting population, any government is in a vulnerable position. This is especially true of upstart dictators or foreign aggressors in the early stages of attempting to establish political control of the society. If one of their key objectives is economic exploitation of the society, then they are in double trouble.

Sanctions

Even the opponents' ability to apply sanctions may on occasion be negatively influenced by nonviolent action. The supply of military or police weapons may be threatened by a foreign country's refusal to sell them, or by strikes in the weapons and munitions factories and transportation system. In some cases the number of agents of repression—police and troops—may be curtailed as the number of volunteers for the military forces declines and potential conscripts refuse duty. Police and troops may carry out orders inefficiently or may refuse them completely—that is, mutiny—potentially leading to nonviolent coercion of the opponents or disintegration of their system of government.

Mutinies and the unreliability of troops in repressing the predominantly nonviolent Russian revolutions of 1905 and February 1917 were highly significant factors in the weakening and final downfall of the tsar's regime. The Nazis recognized that if they lost control of the army their power would be drastically weakened. Goebbels revealed that in early February 1938 the Nazis most feared not a coup d'état but the collective resignation of all high-ranking military officers.

During the East German Rising of 1953, police sometimes withdrew or willingly gave up their weapons. Some East German soldiers mutinied. Even some Soviet soldiers were sympathetic, as evidenced by reports that a thousand Soviet officers and others refused to fire at demonstrators and that fifty-two Communist Party members and soldiers were shot for disobedience after the collapse of the rising. Reports that the Soviets had to replace all of their initial invasion force in Czechoslovakia in 1968 after only a few days further demonstrate the capacity of nonviolent action to weaken the reliability of the opponents' troops and, therewith, the opponents' capacity to apply sanctions. This power potential, if developed and enhanced, may be highly important in future struggles against usurpations and invasions.

Failure or Success?

No type of struggle or action is guaranteed to produce success in the short term every time it is used. This is especially true if no consideration is given to how the means of action are applied, the circumstances of their use, and the degree to which the requirements for effectiveness are fulfilled.

The improvised nonviolent struggles of the past have varied widely in the degree to which they succeeded or failed to reach their avowed objectives. The struggles have also varied in the degree to which the apparently unsuccessful conflicts contributed to the gaining of their objectives at a later date. The record, however, includes significantly more cases of full and partial success than are generally recognized. Among those successes can be counted both small and large campaigns in which nonviolent struggle was the sole or the predominant technique.

These successes include the gaining of de facto independence for most of the American colonies before the War of Independence; the collapse of the tsarist system of Imperial Russia in February 1917; the defeat of the Kapp Putsch and preservation of the Weimar Republic in 1920; the saving of 1,500 Jewish men in Berlin in 1943 by their wives' protests; the rejection of fascist control of schools in 1942 by Norwegian teachers and the general population; the ousting of the dictators of El Salvador and Guatemala in 1944; the defeat of the military coup in Bolivia in 1978; the defeat of the Algiers generals' coup in 1961; the ouster of military dictators in the Sudan in 1964 and 1985; the ousting of the military regime and return to constitutional democracy in Thailand in 1973; the defeat of election fraud and ouster of President Marcos in the Philippines in 1986; the relegalization of Solidarity, the restoration of reasonably free elections, and the selection of a Solidarity Prime Minister in Poland in 1989, and the sudden democratization in late 1989 of East Germany, Bulgaria, and Czechoslovakia. Many other cases could be cited that have been significant in the advancement of popular control over rulers.

While not the only factor, nonviolent struggle also has played a very significant role in a series of other major changes in domestic and international situations. These include the extension of religious liberties in Britain and Massachusetts in the seventeenth and eighteenth centuries; the struggle against slavery in the United States prior to the Civil War; the recognition of labor unions and improvements in wages and working conditions; the gaining of universal manhood suffrage, especially in Sweden and Belgium around the turn of the century; the securing of voting rights for women in the United States and Britain; the saving of the lives of many Jews from the Holocaust during the Second World War, especially in Bulgaria, Denmark, Norway, Belgium, and France; the abolition of legalized racial segregation in the United States; the gaining of independence for India, Pakistan, and Ghana; the gaining of rights of emigration for Soviet Jews in the 1970s; the movement for "civilianization" of government in Brazil in the 1970s and 1980s; and the growth of African economic power in South Africa through strikes, the organization of African trade unions, and economic boycotts in the 1970s and 1980s.

"Success" has been used here to indicate the achievement of substantive objectives by a party in a conflict. This is quite independent of ability to inflict casualties and destruction on opponents. "Failure" then indicates that the substantive objectives have not been achieved. As in other types of conflicts, partial successes and partial failures also of course occur.

In addition to measuring success or failure in attaining objectives, one should also examine two other factors. These are the (1) increases and decreases in the absolute and relative power of the contending groups and (2) changes in the wider influence of and sympathy for each group and its objectives. These factors may contribute to a settlement of unresolved issues in the future, which also may, or may not, bring to fruition the original goals of an earlier nonviolent struggle.

Failure of nonviolent action may be caused by weaknesses in the group employing the technique, by the group not fulfilling important requirements for effectiveness, by its acting in ways that undermine the operation of the technique, by its capitulating or turning to violence in the face of repression, or by neglecting to develop and apply effective strategy and tactics. These factors are similar to those that contribute to defeat in military action, except that in cases of nonviolent struggle the opponents' overwhelming military capacity need not be so influential.

If the group using nonviolent action does not possess sufficient internal strength, determination, ability, and related qualities to make nonviolent action effective, then repetition of phrases and words like "non-violence" will not save it. There is no substitute for genuine strength and skill in applying nonviolent action. If the nonviolent group does not possess these qualities in sufficient quantity to cope with its opponents, the group is unlikely to win.

On the other hand, if the nonviolent fighters are determined, use intelligently chosen strategies and tactics, skillfully act to advance their cause, fulfill the requirements for the working of the technique, and are able to persist in the face of repression, then victory is possible. Such success is likely to have significant advantages over victory by violence. These advantages include fuller and more lasting achievement of the objectives, more equitable power relationships, greater understanding and perhaps even respect between the former contending parties, and increased ability to defend the gains from future attackers or oppressors.

Of the four main examples given in Chapter One, the resistance to the Kapp Putsch and to the coup d'état in Algiers were both fully successful. Both attempts to seize control of the state apparatus and impose new governments and policies were defeated, with the perpetrators' efforts simply dissolving in the face of nonviolent resistance.

The *Ruhrkampf* against the Franco-Belgian invasion and occupation produced mixed results, and only after some time. The withdrawal did not come immediately in response to nonviolent resistance, but only after it had weakened and been called off by the German government. On the other hand, the invasion forces did finally withdraw and the Rhineland was not separated from Germany. With the aid of international intervention from Britain and the United States, the German reparations payments continued, but at a highly reduced rate more approximate to what Germany could afford to pay. The Poincaré government, which had launched the invasion, admitted its failure to gain its objectives. It had been responsible for such brutal repression that many French people came to sympathize with the Germans, who had very recently been enemies in war. The Poincaré government was defeated in the next national election.

The Czechoslovak case was in the end a defeat. In April 1969, the Dubček reform-minded group was removed from the leadership of the Communist Party and the government, being replaced by the more compliant Husak leadership. However, even with the compromise in the Moscow negotiations discussed earlier, the change in leadership had taken the Soviets eight months to achieve, instead of the few days they had reportedly envisaged. Significantly, the Soviets, backed by a half million troops, had to shift from direct military action to slower political manipulations, working with sympathetic sections of the Czechoslovak Communist Party to gain one limited point after another. In the end, the collapse of the resistance leadership in face of a Soviet ultimatum (made after anti-Russian riots in April, which may have been staged) was a more significant factor in the defeat than any loss of will or capacity by the populace. The economic and political costs had been high for both sides. Significantly, however, both sides had been spared the high cost of death and destruction that would have inevitably followed a Czechoslovakian military resistance. Discouragement and disillusionment among Czechs and Slovaks was also part of the price paid. However, the population survived with its honor intact to be able to move again at a later date toward greater human rights and democratic freedoms. Indeed in late 1989, Czechs and Slovaks forced the collapse of Communist one-party rule through massive protest and defiance. The previously jailed dissident, Vaclav Havel, was installed as president and the once-deposed Alexander Dubček was elected chairman of the National Parliament.

Sometimes, the results of nonviolent action have been a "draw" or an interim settlement, exhibiting characteristics of an accommodation. At the end of the 1930–1931 independence campaign in India, formal negotiations took place between Mohandas Gandhi, representing the Indian National Congress, and Lord Irwin, the Viceroy, representing the British government. The result was known as the Gandhi-Irwin Pact. It contained provisions that were seen as advantageous to both the British and the Indians, although it clearly did not represent an Indian victory.

In other cases, a fuller, though still incomplete, victory may be achieved. The struggle then may be terminated with negotiation and a formal agreement. In some cases, the opponents may, without a formal settlement, simply institute or accept changes desired by the nonviolent resisters. The opponents might then even deny that the shifts in policy had anything to do with the resistance. In extreme cases, the opponents' regime may completely collapse or disintegrate as a result of the withdrawal of the sources of power as already noted.

In the long run, the most significant result of nonviolent struggle is likely to be its impact on the resolution of the issues at stake, on the attitudes of the groups toward each other, and on the distribution of power between and within the contending groups. In more extreme situations, acceptable results will be measured only by drastic alteration in the nature of the opponents' policies or system of government, or in its full defeat or disintegration. The latter is especially true in cases involving extreme systems of oppression and dictatorship and of attempted internal usurpations and international aggression.

Changes in the Struggle Group

Participation in nonviolent action is likely to have several important effects on the people taking part. As is true of groups engaged in other types of conflict, the group using nonviolent action tends to become more unified, to improve its internal cooperation, and to increase its feelings of solidarity.

Participation in nonviolent action both requires and produces important psychological and attitudinal changes within the nonviolent group. These may include increased self-esteem, self-respect, and self-confidence, and reduced fear and submissiveness. There appear to be special qualities in nonviolent action that contribute to these results. As people learn about and experience this technique, they may also gain greater awareness of their own power and increased confidence in their ability to influence the course of events. If the nonviolent struggle is conducted reasonably competently, the participants are also likely to become more skilled in the formulation and implementation of strategies and tactics, more capable of maintaining nonviolent discipline in the course of the struggle, and more able to see the conflict through difficult periods. The internal strength of a resisting society and the tenacity of its loci of power are also likely to grow.

These changes in the nonviolent resisters, the grievance group, and the society at large are likely to have important influences on the opponents and the course of the conflict. These are precisely the sort of changes that are detrimental to any type of dictatorship, of either domestic or foreign origin.

Even against Dictatorships

Aristotle pointed out that a tyrant "wants his subjects to have no mutual confidence, no power, little spirit." This is the opposite of the situation produced by participation in nonviolent struggle, as has been demonstrated in case after case. Despite the measures taken by tyrants to deny the subjects those capacities and to gain approval as a supposedly benevolent ruler, Aristotle concluded, "Still, oligarchy and tyranny are shorter-lived than any other constitution." Had more attention been paid to that insight over the centuries, and particularly in recent decades, we would now have a deeper understanding of the reasons for the relatively short duration of dictatorships. With that understanding, people could have further explored how to exacerbate the weaknesses of dictatorships. Had that been done, it is likely that humanity would now be much further along in developing the capacity to

prevent and destroy dictatorships and oppression and to gain and preserve human freedom and justice.

Dictatorships are not as omnipotent as their leaders would have us
believe. Instead, dictatorships contain inherent weaknesses that contribute to their inefficiency, reduce the thoroughness of their controls,
and limit their longevity. At least seventeen such weaknesses have
been identified. These include routinization of the operation of the system; erosion of ideology; inadequate or incorrect information received
from below by the rulers; inefficiency in the operation of all aspects of
the system; internal conflicts among the leadership; restlessness among
intellectuals and students; an apathetic or skeptical public; accentua-
tion of regional, class, cultural, or national differences; competition
among the political police or military forces with the ruling group;
overconcentration of decision making; and the problem faced by all
governments of securing a high degree of reliable cooperation and obedience from the general population.

These weaknesses, and others, can be pinpointed and resistance can
be concentrated on those "cracks in the monolith." Nonviolent struggle is much more suited to that task than is violence.

As the historical record shows, nonviolent struggle has been used
against dictatorships, even very extreme ones, in the form of protests,
resistance, uprisings, disruptions, and revolutions. These have occurred in Latin America and Asia, in Nazi-occupied countries, in Com-
munist-ruled Eastern European countries, in the Soviet Union, and in
China.

The conditions for nonviolent struggle in such cases were difficult
not only because of the repressive political circumstances. Limited
knowledge of this technique, lack of preparation, and the almost complete absence of training have greatly compounded the difficulties. In
addition, nonviolent action has also been commonly, used amidst conditions of great confusion and in the face of unexpected crises or
known terror.

The fact that such cases have occurred in the past suggests that nonviolent struggle will be used again in the future. Even the would-be
tyrants to come will never be able to free themselves from dependence
upon the society they would rule.

Nonviolent struggle in the future is likely to have greater success to
the degree that the participants have advance knowledge of the requirements and strategic principles that make this technique more effective. Struggles conducted with increased knowledge and preparation should be much less difficult than the improvised cases of the past.
However, the many problems in conducting these future struggles and

in developing strategies that people can use to disintegrate well-established dictatorships require urgent, careful attention. The massacre of hundreds of protesters in China in June 1989 is a reminder that all dictatorships do not fall easily, even when faced with massive popular repudiation.

Gaining and dispersing knowledge of the methods of nonviolent struggle, solving the problems of resistance, developing wise strategies, and launching programs of preparation and training are therefore major components of the task of developing a post-military defense policy, a policy that can deter and defend against both internal and external attacks and that can prevent the establishment of new dictatorships in any form.

Notes

For a full account and analysis of the nature of nonviolent struggle, with supporting evidence and documentation for the analysis and points made in this chapter, see Gene Sharp, *The Politics of Nonviolent Action* (Boston: Porter Sargent, 1973), pp. 63–817. This book includes analyses of characteristics, methods, and dynamics, including the process of political jiujitsu and three of the mechanisms of change. The separation of "disintegration" from "nonviolent coercion" occurred following its publications.

Most of the examples briefly cited in this chapter are taken from *The Politics of Nonviolent Action*. When there is no specific reference given for a case cited in this chapter, the reader is referred to the index and footnotes of *The Politics of Nonviolent Action* (hereafter TPONA). Quotations from that volume are cited here by the page number and the footnote number so that the original source can be located more easily. Occasionally, the full original source is included here. The order of references here follows that in the text.

For an account of the Salvadoran case, see Patricia Parkman, *Nonviolent Insurrection in El Salvador: The Fall of Maximiliano Hernández Martínez* (Tucson: University of Arizona Press, 1988).

For a short account of the Guatemalan case, see TPONA, pp. 90–93.

On the Hungarian writers' memorandum, see TPONA, p. 125, n. 33.

On the women's suffrage demonstration, see TPONA, p. 126, n. 39.

On action by the Bulgarian Jews, see TPONA, p. 153, n. 178. The source is Matei Yulzari, "The Bulgarian Jews in the Resistance Movement," in Yuri Suhl, *They Fought Back: The Story of Jewish Resistance in Nazi Europe* (New York: Crown Publishers, 1967), pp. 277–278.

The source on the Brazilian demonstrations is Maria Elena Alves, lecture at the Program on Nonviolent Sanctions, Center for International Affairs, Harvard University, March 16, 1986.

On the Czech newspaper boycott, see TPONA, p. 222 n. 21, and Josef Korbel, *The Communist Subversion of Czechoslovakia 1938–1948*, (Princeton, N.J.: Princeton University Press, 1959).

For information on the East Berlin demonstration, see the *New York Times*, November 5, 1989, p. 1. On the Prague demonstration, see the *New York Times*, November 26, 1989, p. 1.

On the two-hour general strike in Czechoslovakia, see the *New York Times*, November 28, 1989, p. A1.

On the "people's inspection" of the state security headquarters in Leipzig, see *Die Zeit* (Hamburg), December 22, 1989, p. 6.

The McCarthy reference on parallel governmental institutions is to Ronald M. McCarthy, "Resistance, Politics and the Growth of Parallel Government in America, 1765–1775," in Walter Conser, Ronald M. McCarthy, David Toscano, and Gene Sharp, editors, *Resistance, Politics and the American Struggle for Independence, 1765–1775* (Boulder, Colo.: Lynne Rienner Publishers, 1986), p. 498. The whole of the chapter, pp. 472–524, is also relevant. See also in the same book, David Ammerman, "The Continental Association: Economic Resistance and Government by Committee," pp. 225–277.

For additional discussion on parallel government, see TPONA, pp. 423–433.

On the Russian 1905 Revolution, see Sidney Harcave, *First Blood: The Russian Revolution of 1905* (New York: Macmillan, 1964, and London: Collier-Macmillan, 1964); Solomon M. Schwartz, *The Russian Revolution of 1905: The Workers' Movement and the Formation of Bolshevism and Menshevism*, trans. by Gertrude Vakar, with a Preface by Leopold H. Haimson (Chicago and London: University of Chicago Press, 1967), especially pp. 129–195. See also Richard Charques, *The Twilight of Imperial Russia* (London: Phoenix House, 1958), pp. 111–139; Leonard Schapiro, *The Communist Party of the Soviet Union* (New York: Random House, 1960, and London: Eyre & Spotiswoode, 1960), pp. 63–70 and 75; Hugh Seton-Watson, *The Decline of Imperial Russia, 1855–1914* (New York: Frederick A. Praeger, and London: Methuen & Co., 1952), pp. 219–260; Bertram D. Wolfe, *Three Who Made a Revolution* (New York: Dial Press, 1948, and London: Thames and Hudson, 1956), pp. 278–336; and Michael Prawdin, *The Unmentionable Nechaev: A Key to Bolshevism* (London: Allen and Unwin, 1961), pp. 147–149.

On the February 1917 Russian Revolution, see especially George Katkov, *Russia 1917: The February Revolution* (New York: Harper & Row, 1967).

On Danish illegal newspapers, see Jeremy Bennett, "The Resistance Against the German Occupation of Denmark 1940–45," in Adam Roberts, editor, *Civilian Resistance as a National Defence* (Harmondsworth, England, and Baltimore, Md.: Penguin Books, 1969), p. 200.

On the 1956–1957 Hungarian Revolution, see, for example *Report of the Special Committee on the Problem of Hungary* (New York: United Nations, General Assembly Official Records, Eleventh Session, Supplement No. 18–A/3592, 1957). On the workers' councils, see especially Hannah Arendt, *On Revolution* (New York: Viking Press, and London: Faber & Faber, 1963).

On the Polish movement since 1980, see, for example, Nicholas Andrews, *Poland, 1980–1981: Solidarity Against the Party* (Washington, D.C.: National Defense University Press, 1985); Madeleine Korbel Albright, *Poland: The Role of the Press in Political Change* (New York: Praeger, 1983); Timothy Garton Ash, *The Polish Revolution: Solidarity 1980–1982* (London: Jonathan Cape, 1983); Ross A. Johnson, *Poland in Crisis* (Santa Monica, Ca.: Rand Corporation, 1982); Leopold Labedz and the staff of *Survey* magazine, editors, *Poland Under Jaruzelski* (New York: Charles Scribner's Sons, 1984); and Jan Joseph Lipski, *KOR: A History of the Workers' Defense Committee in Poland, 1976–1981* (Berkeley, Los Angeles, and London: University of California Press, 1985).

On the role of fearlessness in France in saving Jews, see TPONA, p. 549, n. 105. The original source is Gerald Reitlinger, *The Final Solution: The Attempt to Exterminate the Jews of Europe 1939–1945* (New York: A. S. Barnes, 1961), p. 328.

On fearlessness in Montgomery, Alabama, and for the Martin Luther King, Jr. quotation, see TPONA, p. 548, nn. 100–101.

On blockage of army tanks in Manila, see Monina Allarey Mercado, editor, *People Power. The Philippine Revolution of 1986. An Eyewitness History* (Manila: James B. Reuter, S. J. Foundation, 1986), chapter five.

On aspects of the Indian 1930–1931 campaign, including the raid at Dharasana, see Gene Sharp, *Gandhi Wields the Weapon of Moral Power: Three Case Histories*, introduced by Albert Einstein (Ahmedabad: Navajivan Publishing House, 1960), pp. 37–226, and S. Gopal, *The Viceroyality of Lord Irwin, 1926–1931* (London: Oxford University Press, 1957), pp. 54–122.

There have as yet been no serious comparative statistical studies of casualty rates between various types of violent conflicts and those in which one side is using nonviolent struggle. A brief discussion of this is contained in TPONA, pp. 583–586, but it is insufficient. Scattered data on the numbers of dead and injured in violent conflicts, when compared to similar data on nonviolent struggles such as those surveyed or cited in this book, suggest that the differences are not only vast but consistently so. It is hoped that someone will undertake such a comparative study soon, taking into consideration various factors, including the scale of the conflict, the numbers of people involved, the nature of the regimes and populations, the types of issues at stake, and others.

On Finnish resistance, see TPONA, pp. 593–594, n. 93. The original citation is to William Robert Miller, *Nonviolence: A Christian Interpretation* (New York: Association Press, 1964), p. 247.

On the repression of nonviolent demonstrators in Prague, see the *New York Times*, December 15, 1989, p. A17.

On the 1924–1925 Vykom satyagraha, see TPONA, pp. 82–83, and references in n. 18. The original sources are Joan V. Bondurant, *Conquest of Violence: The Gandhian Philosophy of Conflict* (Princeton, N.J.: Princeton University Press, 1958), pp. 46–52; Mohandas K. Gandhi, *Non-violent Resistance* (New York: Schocken Books, 1967), Indian edition, *Satyagraha* (Ahmedabad: Navajivan Publishing House, 1951) pp. 177–203; and Mahadev Desai, *The Epic of Travancore* (Ahmedabad: Navajivan, 1937).

An introductory discussion of strategic principles in nonviolent struggle is presented in TPONA, pp. 492–510.

On the Peshawar evacuation, see TPONA, pp. 335, 432, 675, and 747, and S. Gopal, *The Viceroyality of Lord Irwin 1926–1931*, pp. 68–69.

On the walkout of Philippine computer operators, see Mercado, *People Power*, pp. 67, 75–76.

On the Norwegian teachers' resistance, see Gene Sharp, "Tyranny Could Not Quell Them," pamphlet (London: Peace News, 1958, and later editions).

On aspects of the 1953 East German Rising, see Stefan Brandt, *The East German Rising* (New York: Praeger, 1957), and Theodor Ebert, "Non-violent Resistance Against Communist Regimes?" in Roberts, *Civilian Resistance as a National Defence*, chapter 8.

On the economic impact of the American colonial noncooperation movements, see Conser et al., *Resistance, Politics, and the American Struggle for Independence*.

On the economic impact of Indian boycotts of British goods, see TPONA, pp. 751–752, nn. 184–189.

On the Arab oil embargo, see Mohammed E. Ahrari, *The Dynamics of Oil Diplomacy: Conflict and Consensus* (New York: Arno Press, 1980), chapter 6, and Sheikh Rustum Ali, *OPEC: The Failing Giant* (Lexington, Ky.: University Press of Kentucky, 1986), chapter 5.

The quotation on the strike against the Kapp Putsch is from S. William Halperin, *Germany Tried Democracy: A Political History of the Reich from 1918 to 1933* (Hamden, Conn.: Archon Books, 1963 [1946]), pp. 179–180.

WIELDING POWER   81

On the Nazi ban on general strikes, see TPONA, p. 532, n. 43. The original reference is to Jacques Delarue, *The Gestapo: A History of Horror* (New York: William Morrow, 1964), p. 8.

On Nazi fear of military resignations, see TPONA, p. 753, n. 192. The source is Walter Görlitz, *History of the German General Staff, 1647–1945*, trans. by Brian Battershaw (New York: Praeger, 1962), p. 319. See also p. 341. On mutinies during the East German Rising, see TPONA, p. 753, n. 194.

On Russian troop morale problems in Czechoslovakia and consequent replacement, see Robert Littell, editor, *The Czech Black Book: Prepared by the Institute of History, Czechoslovak Academy of Sciences* (New York: Praeger, 1969), pp. 212–213.

The quotations from Aristotle are from *The Politics*, trans. by T. A. Sinclair, revised by Trevor J. Saunders (Harmondsworth, England, and Baltimore, Md.: Penguin Books, 1983 [1981]), pp. 227 and 353.

The phrase "cracks in the monolith" is from Karl Deutsch. See his essay, "Cracks in the Monolith," in Carl J. Friedrich, editor, *Totalitarianism* (Cambridge, Mass.: Harvard University Press, 1954), pp. 308–333.

On weaknesses of dictatorial systems see also Gene Sharp, "Facing Dictatorships With Confidence," in *Social Power and Political Freedom* (Boston: Porter Sargent, 1980), pp. 91–112, and the sources cited there.

Four

Civilian-based Defense

Developing a New Defense Policy

CIVILIAN STRUGGLES of noncooperation and defiance have been conducted for a variety of objectives, ranging from the granting of voting rights to the toppling of dictators. As shown in Chapter One, such struggles have also been improvised, as official national defense policy, by Germany, France, and Czechoslovakia, against both internal and foreign attackers.

This chapter focuses on whether—and if so, how—defense by civilian resistance can be made a realistic choice for the coming decades. Security threats are likely to be with us for a long time, and military defense options will continue to suffer serious limitations and disadvantages for those who would defend their liberties, self-determination, and chosen social systems. Therefore, civilian-based defense merits careful and rigorous analysis.

We will consider how to combine the disparate methods of nonviolent action in more refined ways, to adapt them specifically to the purposes of deterrence and national defense, and to enrich their application with new knowledge, insight, strategy, and preparation. With the benefit of additional research, policy studies, strategic analyses, contingency planning, and training, it would be possible to develop for consideration a refined, coherent policy, with multiple strategic options. The cumulative result would be to multiply the effectiveness of civilian-based defense. It should not be too difficult to produce an effective power (conservatively estimated) at least ten times greater than that demonstrated in the most powerful of the past cases of improvised nonviolent struggle.

This chapter presents the outlines of a deliberately developed, post-military defense policy. With such a policy in place and operational, the population of a country will be ready to resist in case of a domestic usurpation or a foreign invasion. Readiness is highly important in building both the deterrent and the defense capacities of this policy.

Aggression for Land or Genocide

Attention to the objectives of the attackers is a crucial factor in the planning of civilian-based defenses. The fact that attackers may have certain extreme objectives such as territorial aggrandizement or genocide, often causes people to dismiss a civilian-based defense policy as naive and useless. However, rigorous examination of the military defense alternatives in such extreme cases will reveal serious grounds for doubts about their utility. Indeed, a defensive war or violent resistance can facilitate mass slaughter and provide to the perpetrators helpful "justifications," such as blaming "war-time necessities" or asserting that their actions were self-defensive measures against "terrorists." The attackers may even claim that their aggression and mass killings were merely regrettable but necessary "preemptive" measures to save *themselves* from intended extermination by their victims.

War-time situations seem to provide the conditions under which weapons intended to depopulate vast territories are more likely to be used, weapons such as poison gasses, chemicals, and biological agents, or neutron nuclear bombs. These could also be used against nonviolent resisters, but there appear to be impediments to such use, and there are no known cases of this type.

In cases of attempted genocide and territorial aggrandizement, long-term dependency on the attacked population and society is obviously not intended by the attackers—eliminating for the attacked population an important leverage in its defense effort. However, there is historical evidence showing that even attackers intent on seizing territory for its own sake or to perpetrate genocide, at certain stages at least, have required the submission and even cooperation of their victims.

The shift, on pragmatic grounds, of German policy in the occupied parts of the Soviet Union from 1940 to 1944—even in wartime—is noteworthy in this respect. The Nazis regarded the Slavic inhabitants of Eastern Europe and the Soviet Union as subhumans, to be driven out or exterminated in order to provide empty territory for German colonization, *Lebensraum* for the German *Volk*. For a long time, therefore, German officials did not even *seek* cooperation from the *Untermenschen* (subhumans). Nevertheless, despite the Nazi ideological position, some German officials and officers reluctantly concluded that in order to maintain control in the "Eastern territories," cooperation was needed from the very population to be exterminated. Many such instances have been cited by Alexander Dallin in his study of the German occupation. For example, Dallin reports that Wilhelm Kube, the *Generalkommissar* in Belorussia, reluctantly conceded in 1942 "that German forces could not exercise effective control without enlisting the population." Dallin quotes a statement by German military commanders in the Soviet Union in December 1942: "The seriousness of the situation clearly makes imperative the positive cooperation of the population. Russia can be beaten only by Russians." General Harteneck wrote in May 1943: "We can master the wide Russian expanse which we have conquered only with the Russians and Ukranians who live in it, never against their will."

Against attempts of genocide, a well-prepared noncooperation campaign can increase the problems of control of the population in the interim stages before genocide could be perpetrated, hence slowing down the process. Against attackers seeking empty land, such resistance could impede effective control of the territories involved. Also, various types of nonviolent action can influence the willingness of those ordered to inflict mass killings. If news spreads of both the intent and the initiation of mass slaughter, there may be time to enlist the aid of the aggressors' home population, other governments, and international bodies to bring a halt to such acts. Unfortunately, newer forms of the technology of killing enable aggressors to speed up the genocidal process once it is launched.

The continued development and exploration of policies to prevent and defeat such atrocities must nevertheless continue, and an attitude of helpless fatalism must be prevented. Research and analysis should include attention to the unique problems involved in nonviolent struggle in these situations. This examination cannot be done here. It should be noted, however, that various types of nonviolent resistance against the Holocaust were used with some success in both Germany and in Nazi-allied or Nazi-occupied countries. Much is still to be learned about how to prevent and defeat genocide and other mass killings.

It is important to recognize that the objectives of territorial aggrandizement and genocide are present in only a clear minority of the attacks against which defense is required. Most cases of internal usurpation and foreign military aggression have different objectives. Hence, the case for civilian-based defense does not stand or fall on the basis of one's judgment about extreme cases. Whatever measures may finally be judged necessary to deal with those situations, an effective civilian-based defense to prevent internal usurpation and foreign invasion and occupation can be developed. It is to these much more common situations that the remainder of this chapter is addressed.

The Attackers' Calculations of Objectives and Success

Both internal usurpations and foreign invasions are intended to achieve some objective. Internal usurpations, by coup d'état or executive takeover, may aim to bring greater power to the individual or group heading them or may have longer-range political, economic, or ideological objectives. Most cases of foreign invasion and occupation are conducted for such purposes as establishing a puppet or subservient government, annexing territory with its population intact, economic exploitation, gaining certain raw materials, extending an ideology or religion to a new population, removing or preempting a perceived military threat, and transporting military equipment and troops to attack a third country.

The success of all such internal or external attacks depends on the achievement of their objectives. They are consequently most likely to be rationally planned acts, rather than spontaneous fits of rage or purposeless displays of massive destruction. For example, the Franco-Belgian invasion of the Ruhr aimed to secure scheduled payments of reparations and to separate the Rhineland from Germany. The Soviet Union in 1968 wanted to restore a rigid Communist system in Czechoslovakia. Internal usurpations always aim to oust the previous government and impose a new one in control of the state apparatus and the society, as in the Kapp Putsch and the French generals' coup. Unless the attackers gain their objectives, they will have lost. They will have to calculate, therefore, how to achieve their goals.

In order for attackers to secure most or all of their objectives, they must also govern the occupied country. If not the prime objective itself, political control is a necessary step toward gaining the attackers' other goals. Economic exploitation, transportation of materials, ideological indoctrination, evacuation of inhabitants—all require a great deal of cooperation and assistance from the people and institutions of the attacked country. It is not sufficient simply to control the country's land. The attackers must also control its population and institutions. The costs of controlling a resisting population may greatly influence the would-be attackers' decision to attack.

Potential attackers usually will calculate the odds for and against achieving their intended goals to determine whether the benefits are worth the anticipated costs. If the chances of success are small, and the costs high, the potential attackers are not likely to attack. They are deterred.

Deterrence by Civilian-based Defense

Deterrence, therefore, is not intrinsically tied to military means, much less to nuclear weapons capacity. Deterrence can occur within the context of strictly nonviolent means.

Whether civilian-based defense can provide deterrence in a specific situation, and the degree to which it does so, will depend on two main factors: (1) the *actual capacity* of the society to deny to the attackers their desired objectives and to impose unacceptable costs (alone or in cooperation with others) and (2) the potential attackers' *perception* of that society's capacity to deny their objectives and impose costs.

Let us look at these factors more closely. In contrast to military means, civilian-based deterrence would not be produced by the threat of massive physical destruction and death on the attackers' homeland. Rather, deterrence would be achieved if the attackers perceive that the attacked society could deny them their goals and impose excessive costs.These costs would include harm to the attackers' regime domestically (internal dissent and disruption), internationally (diplomatic and economic costs), and in the attacked country itself (denial of objectives, blockage of effective political controls, and inducement of disaffection among the attackers' troops, functionaries, and population). In other words, *the deterrence capacity of civilian-based defense is based directly upon an actual defense capacity*. This contrasts with both nuclear and large-scale conventional military deterrence capacities, which today can often effectively *avenge* after attacks but rarely *defend* against attack (meaning to protect one's population, way of life, and institutions). The military weapons that are to be used are far too destructive to provide the civilian society with protection.

Beyond the initial period of research, policy development and evaluation, and feasibility studies, two crucial elements are required to produce a deterrence capacity by civilian-based defense. The first of these elements is intensive preparation and training for the whole population and all its institutions. At times this preparation may be accompanied by institutional and social change (generally toward increased devolution of power and greater acceptance of responsibility by individuals, groups, and institutions). The aim of these changes is to enhance the resilience, self-reliance, and resistance capacity of the society. This includes the defenders' ability to prevent the attackers from consolidating political control and the capacity to deny attackers any other objectives. The defense capacity will also include the ability to increase drastically the costs to the attackers of such a venture and to multiply the domestic and international problems that can be imposed on the attackers.

The second requirement is a program to communicate to all possible attackers an accurate perception of the powerful defense capacity that can be mobilized under the new defense policy. Given a genuinely powerful and prepared defense capacity, publicity—not merely openness—about it will increase the deterrent effect on both internal usurpations and foreign invasions.

As noted in Chapter One, deterrence is a crucial part of the much broader process of dissuasion of attack. Dissuasion may additionally include the influences of rational argument, moral appeal, distraction, and nonprovocative policies. If the country wishes to discourage attacks on itself, in addition to building up its civilian-based deterrence capacity, it will do well to gain for itself respect and sympathy from people in other countries. This may be achieved through positive perceptions of the kind of society the country is, or is becoming, and through the kind of foreign relations it conducts. Certain types of foreign assistance, emergency relief efforts, and other positive international relations may be among these measures. Together, these policies may result in less hostility against and more good will for countries employing a civilian-based defense. While not necessarily decisive, these policies could in some circumstances reduce the chances of attack. However, such policies alone are unlikely to be sufficient. An adequate capacity to defend the society if it is nevertheless attacked is also essential.

A civilian-based *forward strategy* is a possible additional means of preventing foreign attacks in certain situations. Such a strategy could be employed against attacks that seek to achieve certain specific objectives—even those that aim to control only limited parts of territory (such as for naval bases, airports, the extraction of mineral resources, and the like)—in ways in which conventional civilian-based strategies are of dubious effectiveness.

In such a case, a civilian-based defense might spread technical "know-how" on the ways dissatisfied groups in the aggressor's homeland (or in other occupied countries) might conduct effective nonviolent resistance, and even massive civilian insurrection. This could be done through radio, television, telephone, printed matter, letters, cassettes, and videos. Resistance and uprisings at home are not favorable circumstances for dispersing troops and functionaries abroad against well-prepared, defense-minded countries.

No deterrent—military or civilian—can ever be guaranteed to deter. Capacity to deal with its possible failure is therefore essential. In contrast to military means, the deterrent capacity of civilian-based defense rests directly upon its capacity to *defend*. Unlike nuclear deterrents, the failure of civilian-based defense preparations to deter does not bring annihilation, but implementation of the real defense capacity for the first time. It is therefore essential that we explore the broad outlines of how that special type of defense could operate.

Fighting Capacity in Civilian-based Defense

As we have seen, the capacity of this policy to defend against an attack rests on the ability to deny the aggressors' objectives and to inflict extensive domestic and international costs. In order to implement civilian-based defense, people must have the will to resist, to prepare well, and to struggle in the face of casualties, just as they do with military means. Potentially, the whole population—regardless of sex and age—and all institutions of the society are participants in the struggle.

In many cases of internal and external attacks, there has been an initial period of confusion, frequently accompanied by a sense of helplessness and lack of direction in the attacked population. This was clearly the case in Norway following the Nazi invasion in April 1940. It took some months for people to realize how, once military resistance had ended, they might resist both Quisling's fascist party, the *Nasjonal Samling*, and the German military occupation backed by the Gestapo. With advance preparation and widespread knowledge of the general guidelines of resistance (including responsibilities and possible roles of various parts of the population and particular institutions), the population would have been much more able to avoid such a sense of uncertainty and confusion and instead would have been able to face the coming crisis with determination, spirit, and confidence.

General opposition and a desire to defend the society against the attackers are insufficient, however. They must be translated into a *grand strategy* of action. This will include the general goals of defense, the issues on which the struggle will concentrate, the choice of the general technique of action, and other broad means that will be used to achieve defense. The formulated grand strategy in turn must be developed into various individual *strategies* of struggle for particular purposes and situations. Each strategy will set forth how a particular campaign will develop and how its separate components will work together. Each will encompass diverse *tactics*, or more restricted plans of action, to achieve limited objectives. Tactics and specific *methods* of action must be chosen carefully so that they contribute to achieving the goals of each particular strategy.

The weapons, or methods, of civilian-based defense are nonviolent ones: psychological, social, economic, and political, as surveyed in Chapter Three. Among those that have been used in past improvised cases of nonviolent struggle are the following: symbolic protests, paralyzing transportation, social boycotts, specific and general strikes, civil disobedience, economic shutdowns, political noncooperation, adoption of false identities, economic boycotts, public demonstrations, slowdowns, publication of banned newspapers, deliberate inefficiency in carrying out orders, assistance to persecuted people, broadcast of resistance radio and television, public defiance by the legislature, judicial resistance, formal governmental opposition, denial of legitimacy to the usurpers, noncooperation by civil servants, legislative procrastination and delay, declarations of defiance, continuation of old policies and laws, student defiance, children's demonstrations, refusal of collaboration, individual and mass resignations, massive and selective disobedience, maintaining the autonomy of independent organizations and institutions, subversion of the usurpers' troops, and incitement to mutiny.

No single blueprint exists or can be created to plan deterrence and defense capacity by civilian-based defense for all situations. That is much more true of civilian means than of military means of conflict. In both conventional military and nuclear conflicts the weapons overwhelmingly destroy and kill in essentially the same ways regardless of the issues at stake in the conflict. In civilian-based defense, however, the political, social, economic, and psychological weaponry applied in any given case should specifically target the issues in contention. The choice of methods, therefore, should be primarily affected by the specific strategies selected to prevent the aggressors' from achieving their goals and by general strategic principles of nonviolent struggle, as noted in Chapter Three.

Maintaining Legitimacy and Capacity for Self-government

A fundamental precept of any sound strategy in civilian-based defense is to maintain the legitimacy and capacity for self-government of the society in the face of the attackers' attempts to impose their own rule. Stated negatively, the defenders must always deny legitimacy to the attackers and prevent them from effectively governing the country, whether the attackers attempt to take over the existing governmental apparatus or to establish their own. The defenders must oppose and defeat both of these aims.

Defense of the political system of the country is crucial even if the attackers' primary objective is not to restructure it on their own model. As previously noted, to achieve almost any objective that takes time to realize, the attackers will have to obtain extensive cooperation from the attacked society's population and institutions. They may attempt to achieve this either by securing the submissive assistance of the existing governmental structure or by imposing a new one to carry out their objectives. It is, therefore, crucial that the population refuse all legitimacy to the attackers and that the existing government be kept from submitting and collaborating. In civilian-based defense it is necessary to keep the attackers from utilizing the defending government's symbolism, legitimacy, administration, and institutions of social and political control, as well as its police and any existing military forces.

When the aggressors seek to establish (or have succeeded in establishing) their own "government," it is vital that the defenders (1) isolate this "government" through various means of noncooperation and

(2) maintain their own governmental forms parallel to those of the aggressors. The defenders' parallel government may retain the old governmental structure if the attackers have been unable to seize it, or the parallel government may take less formally organized forms. In either case, this parallel government should operate alongside the ostracized structures created by the attackers.

Parallel government was discussed in Chapter Three, where the examples were primarily cases that had occurred in revolutionary situations. Here, instead, the focus is on maintaining the moral and legal authority of a system that has been attacked and keeping effective institutions of governance outside of the control of the attackers, be they internal usurpers or foreign invaders. Definitive analysis of parallel governments and careful examination of their role in civilian-based defense struggles have not yet been undertaken. However, a survey of various examples suggests that the maintenance of an autonomous legitimate government is highly important in preventing would-be usurpers or foreign invaders from gaining political control.

In both the German and the French cases of defense against coups d'état described in Chapter One, the legitimate government survived fully, or in some limited form, throughout the conflict. Even though the Ebert government fled from Berlin and the capital was occupied, the highest officials retained their positions and the governments of the provinces were never replaced. With the bureaucracy and various governmental agencies obeying the legitimate government, the putschists were left with little control. In the French case, the de Gaulle–Debré government in Paris was never toppled, due to various factors. This was crucial to the final collapse of the coup in Algiers. Even there, the rebels' initial hold on the governmental apparatus soon eroded. The continued existence of the government of the Weimar Republic during the Franco-Belgian occupation of the Ruhr was also vital in establishing and supporting the noncooperation policy.

During the Second World War, several governments-in-exile located in London played significant parallel roles. They both served as alternative institutions of legitimacy—in contrast to the collaborationist regimes established under the German occupation—and at times assisted resistance movements in the home countries. The Norwegian government-in-exile, for example, managed to get money into occupied Norway to support families of arrested nonviolent resisters, and the Netherlands' government issued calls for the Dutch railway workers to initiate a strike in September 1944 (which lasted into 1945) to assist the Allied invasion of Europe.

In the Czechoslovak case in 1968–1969, the government and Communist Party initially followed a policy of complete noncooperation with the Soviet occupation. This *initial* response is exemplary. During this period, the Soviets were never able to establish even the semblance of a new government. It can be said that the ultimate failure of the Czechoslovak defense struggle began with the willingness of government and party officials to compromise with the Soviets in the Moscow negotiations, especially in legitimizing the presence of Warsaw Pact occupation troops in the country. This was followed by bit-by-bit concessions to the Soviets over the ensuing months, until the final capitulation to Soviet demands in April 1969 to replace the Dubček leadership. In short, uncompromising leadership from the pre-invasion political structure existed only for a week or so at the beginning of the struggle. Effective nonviolent struggle for defense was waged as long as the established government maintained its legitimate role despite the presence of the Soviet military command. Defiance of the occupation forces and potential Stalinist collaborators by the established political system was vital. The Soviet failure to gain its political objectives through military might forced them to shift to gradualist political pressures, to which the Czechoslovak leadership succumbed.

Selecting Strategies for Defense

In addition to keeping the attackers from seizing control of the political system, it is essential to make great efforts to deny the attackers any additional goals they may have. If the attackers' aims are, for example, economic exploitation, the most appropriate strategies and methods of defense are likely to be economic, and will differ from the means of defense appropriate if the attackers' aims were political, ideological, territorial, genocidal, or other.

For example, in their invasion France and Belgium aimed, among other things, to exploit the coal reserves of the Ruhr. Hence, a significant part of the Germans' defense efforts focused on denying the occupiers access to the vast coal reserves. Miners' strikes, occupation of the mines, boycotts by transport workers, and the like were high among the important methods of resistance used.

On the other hand, the issue may be political. The point in contention at any given moment may be a fairly limited one, as in the previously noted Norwegian case of keeping the schools out of fascist control. In that case, the primary methods of resistance were forms of social and political noncooperation as well as various forms of wider symbolic protest and intervention (including the conducting of improvised school classes in private homes).

As discussed earlier, the initial Russian aim in Czechoslovakia was also political, but on a grand scale: to replace the Dubček party and government leadership with a compliant Stalinist group. Consequently, the resistance focused initially to a large degree on preventing the formation of a collaborationist government of Stalinists, employing extremely strong psychological, social, and political pressures.

With civilian-based defense planning, defenders can pinpoint potential attackers' likely objectives and their strategies, enabling the defenders to devise counterstrategies and options *before* an attack occurs. Planning can also lead to the development of alternative strategies and contingency plans that would allow defenders to maintain the initiative in a civilian-based defense struggle. All these strategic analyses in peacetime would greatly maximize the defenders' power under wartime conditions.

The choice of civilian-based defense strategies and the means for implementing them ought also to be influenced by the following factors (not in order of importance):

> the nature of the attacking regime or group;
> the degree to which the two sides feel close to, or alien from, each other in other relationships;
> the nature of the attackers' means of action and repressive measures;
> the degree to which third parties can influence or pressure the attackers;
> the degree to which the defenders can be influenced by third parties;
> the internal strength of the attacked society and its non-state institutions;
> the vulnerability of the attackers' regime and system;
> the degree and nature of the advance preparations for defending the society;
> the relative importance of the issues at stake for the attackers and defenders;
> the vulnerability or self-reliance of the defending society economically, especially for food, water, and fuel; and
> the willingness of the defenders to sustain casualties as the price of defense.

The civilian defenders will also need to consider which mechanism of change is most likely to achieve victory, as discussed in Chapter Three. The defenders may wish to convert the attackers to the view that both their objectives and the attack itself are unjustified. The defenders may be willing to accommodate, as is done in most strikes. However, compromise with one's attackers is not a laudatory objective for most defense struggles. Instead, the defenders may aim to coerce the attackers into abandoning both their original goals and the attack itself.

In special cases, coercion will be insufficient. When the foreign attackers' home regime has oppressed its own people and is in a precarious condition, the aim might be not only to coerce it into withdrawing its troops from the defending country, but also, in cooperation with resisters in the attackers' homeland, to force its disintegration. Or, when the attack is an internal usurpation, the aim should be to secure its dissolution. The attacking group should not survive as a political unit, even one that is willing to capitulate. There should remain no surviving organized part of that group able to make a similar attempt in the future.

In practice, the mechanisms of conversion, accommodation, and nonviolent coercion are intimately blended, as mentioned earlier, and disintegration may result from a mixture of conversion and nonviolent coercion. A preference for one mechanism or another will, however, strongly affect the choice of the grand strategy for defense and also of the particular methods of action applied.

Care may be required in determining what other types of action might be used with nonviolent struggle in a civilian-based defense. The answer is not determined simply by asking whether the action is "violent" or "nonviolent." Those are but two special categories within a wider range of other, clearly distinguishable types of action, including destruction of property. While the issue of the compatibility of these means with civilian-based defense is clearly important, the answer is not always obvious.

There appears to be little or no problem with some of these activities that fall between military resistance and nonviolent struggle. For example the removal of key parts from machinery or vehicles, the removal or release in safe ways of fuel for vehicles, the removal or destruction, in ways not risking lives, of records and files or computer information of government departments and agencies (as the police). Also, damage or destruction of one's own property to prevent it from being seized or used in the future by attackers—such as demolishing key bridges or tunnels to block an invading army—seems to be compatible with civilian-based defense.

Clearly very dangerous to the effectiveness of nonviolent struggle, however, is demolition and destruction of machinery, transport, buildings, bridges, installations, and the like where these actions in any degree risk injury or death. This judgment is not necessarily ethical but pragmatic. While further examination of the evidence and issues is merited, this type of act appears to be at best extremely risky and at worst highly counterproductive for civilian-based defense. As experience in the 1923 *Ruhrkampf* seems to show, this type of sabotage may kill not only troops and other persons serving the attackers but also one's own people. In addition, it may contribute to extreme repression, tend to shift the basis of the struggle from nonviolent resistance to destruction of property, and reduce sympathy and support for the resisters. In the *Ruhrkampf*, this type of sabotage helped to undermine the previously stronger nonviolent resistance. Demolitions and similar acts are therefore generally best excluded from the armory of civilian-based defense.

Not all civilian-based defense struggles will be equally successful, and there is no formula that, if followed, will guarantee victory. However, it is possible to indicate broadly that the effectiveness of civilian-based defense will depend on at least seven factors (again not listed in order of importance):

the population's will to defend against the attack;

the internal strength of the attacked society;

the ability of the population and institutions to retain control of their sources of power and to deny them to the attackers;

the strategic wisdom exercised by the defenders;

the ability of the defenders to deny to the attackers their objectives;

the capacity of the civilian defenders to fulfill the requirements for effective nonviolent struggle, including the maintenance of nonviolent discipline and resistance despite repression; and

the defenders' skill in aggravating the weaknesses of the attackers' system and regime.

Resisting the Aggressors' Violence

People will need the knowledge of how to endure the pressures of struggle and also the strength to persist despite repression. They will need to know how to transform significant intermediate triumphs into lasting final successes. Understanding, planning, and concerted informed action will enable the defending population to mobilize their power potential and maximize their defense capacity.

The success of nonviolent methods hinges to a large degree upon persistence in their application despite repression and upon maintenance of nonviolent discipline in the face of provocations. A shift to violence would alter the conflict from an asymmetrical one of nonviolent against violent weapons (which has great advantages for the civilian defenders) to a symmetrical one in which both sides are using violent weapons (which generally accords greater advantage to the better-equipped attackers).

Repression against civilian defenders may be harsh. Resisters, family, and friends may be arrested, tortured, and killed. Whole population groups may be denied food, water, or fuel. Demonstrators, strikers, and obstructive civil servants may be shot. Mayors, city councilors, teachers, and clergy may be sent to concentration camps. Hostages may be executed. Protesters may even be massacred. The human costs of defense must not be underestimated. The casualties and other sacrifices involved in civilian-based defense must, however, be placed in the context of the vastly higher costs of both conventional and guerrilla wars, to say nothing of nuclear war. Suffering and death are virtually inevitable in any case of acute struggle. Nonviolent struggles, however, tend to *minimize* casualties and destruction. As noted in Chapter Three, the casualty rates for dead and wounded appear from limited available evidence to be but a small fraction of those in roughly comparable conventional wars, and especially of those in guerrilla wars.

As in any major conflict, including military wars, flight or capitulation in the face of the attackers' violence is an unacceptable response. The civilian defenders must not be surprised by severe repression and brutalities. When these occur, the defenders must not cease their resistance. Repression is often a reaction to the recognition that the resistance is indeed imperiling the success of the attack. Any attempt to halt the attackers' violence, however brutal, by diminishing or ceasing resistance will only teach the attackers to repeat such violence even more severely in the future, for it produced the desired result: submission.

While the defenders may shift to other methods of nonviolent action that challenge the attackers in different ways, the defenders must not capitulate to violence. When casualties occur in nonviolent struggles, they can bring the process of political jiujitsu into operation, which in many cases can be crucial in achieving success.

Two Strategies for the Initial Stage

No single blueprint can be designed for every civilian-based struggle. It is possible, however, to outline some of the likely main components and strategies of most civilian-based defenses.

When both the deterrent effect of civilian-based defense preparations and the dissuasive effects of other domestic and foreign policies have failed to prevent an invasion or internal usurpation, it is time to put the defense policy into operation. Some type of defense strategy must be applied immediately in the first stage of the attack. It is very important that the attacked society make major efforts to seize the initiative in the struggle and not simply respond to acts of the attackers.

The initial strategies of the defenders are likely to take one of two main forms, one designed to communicate the defenders' will to resist and to warn of powerful future struggle, and the other, while also communicative, planned to demonstrate in action some of the stronger types of resistance that are likely to be used at a later stage.

As developed strategies, neither has exact historical precedents, although particular elements of each have occurred in past cases. In Czechoslovakia in 1968, for example, various initial methods were used that are here incorporated as elements of both strategies. They included people linking hands to block bridges that Soviet troop carriers needed to cross, passing out leaflets to Soviet soldiers, symbolic strikes, defiant declarations by the National Assembly, and stopping the movement of Soviet tanks in Prague by surrounding them with masses of people. A combination of methods used as part of a well-planned civilian-based defense is likely to give these strategies far greater impact than the initial actions taken in any past cases of improvised nonviolent resistance for defense.

The strategy of communication and warning is not designed primarily as resistance itself but as simple communication. This strategy is addressed first and foremost to the attackers but also to third parties and even to one's own people. By means of words and symbolic acts, the attackers are informed that the society will be defended by a determined, well-prepared, civilian-based defense on a large scale. This strategy may be more appropriate against a foreign invasion than a coup d'état or executive usurpation, against which strong noncooperation and defiance may be required from the very beginning. Important elements of this strategy could, however, be combined with massive noncooperation.

Initial action using a strategy of communication and warning will be relatively mild, as compared to later strategies of noncooperation and defiance, but that does not mean that this action is insignificant. This communication of the intent to wage strong nonviolent resistance in the future can be compared to the cocking and aiming of a pistol being mild in relation to the subsequent firing.

The strategy of "nonviolent blitzkrieg" may, in contrast to the communication strategy, take the form of a dramatic demonstration of massive nonviolent resistance and defiance, probably combined with some of the methods of the communication strategy. The "blitzkrieg" strategy is appropriate against internal usurpations and, on occasion, foreign invasion or a coup supported by foreign troops.

This nonviolent blitzkrieg would take such forms as large-scale repudiation of the attackers' authority, general strikes, massive political noncooperation, widespread appeals to the attackers' troops, and similar methods (developed more fully below). The odds that the attackers might be shocked into a quick retreat by the clear demonstration of solidarity are usually quite small, but favorable in special circumstances. In any case, the blitzkrieg strategy will communicate to all concerned that the attack will be met by a determined defense

The Strategy of Communication and Warning

In this strategy, the civilian defenders will seek by words and actions to convey the message that a vigorous and powerful defensive struggle will be waged, of a type especially difficult to counteract and defeat.

Some of this communication will be aimed at the leaders of the attackers. They may not have included in their calculations the strong will of the population to resist the attack. The attackers also may not have taken seriously the power of civilian-based defense, especially if this happens to be one of the early well-prepared applications of the policy. If either is the case, there may still be a small chance to correct the attackers' misperceptions and to induce them to halt the attack, perhaps with some face-saving excuse.

In the case of invasion, some of the warning and communication will also be aimed directly and indirectly at the general population of the attackers' home country. In the case of coup d'état, the warning would be directed within one's own society. In either case, it may be necessary to correct lies the population has been told about the attack. Because officials of one's own government or military forces may be involved in a usurpation, or may have "invited" foreign military intervention (the Soviets attempted to use this excuse initially in Czechoslovakia), it is important that people are able to distinguish and resist unconstitutional and illegitimate acts by their own "leaders." This is more likely to occur where the defenders use nonviolent rather than military means. In the past people have sometimes passively submitted to a military coup primarily because they wished to avoid a civil war.

Words and actions to communicate the intent to defend and the means by which the defense will be conducted will also be aimed at one's neighboring countries, the general international community, and, in cases of civilian-based defense treaty organizations, at one's allies. This communication will lay the groundwork for (a) helpful kinds of aid to the attacked country; (b) the avoidance of actions that would harm the defense; and (c) facilitation of international diplomatic, moral, economic, and political pressures against the attackers.

Communications and warnings addressed to the attackers will also be heard by one's own people. Descriptions of the defense to be offered will also be important for sections of the population that may have been little involved in or inadequately informed about the defense policy. (Where civilian-based defense has been adequately prepared, this will not be as important.)

Radio, television, newspapers, and leaflets may be used directly by national and local leadership to communicate directly with the defending population. While not planned in advance, radio, television, and resistance newspapers were all used in the early days of the invasion and occupation of Czechoslovakia. The radio broadcasts, which helped to guide the population in its nonviolent resistance, were credited with being highly significant. With benefit of advance planning and preparation, all these means of communication will be especially important.

Whether through communications addressed to the attackers or aimed at one's own population, the people will hear much more than the news of the attack. They will also receive the message that their whole society is becoming involved in a vitally important defensive struggle, and that they have an important role to play in it. This message will support specific preparations and actions in their neighborhoods and places of work and can contribute to the growth of the spirit of resistance in the population as a whole.

During this period, domestic sympathizers with the attackers and persons who may opportunistically seek to enrich themselves or to gain positions of power, will need to be warned. By words and actions, they will be told both that strong defense will be offered by the whole society and that (while no physical harm will be done to them) collaborators will become targets of persistent resistance. They will be regarded as betrayers of their own people and be prevented from retaining any rewards from the attackers.

The attackers' troops and functionaries will be especially important targets during this stage of the struggle. They may have been told lies about the situation in the defending country, about what to expect from the population, or even about what country they have invaded. One of the key ways to dissolve the attempted takeover or occupation is to reduce or take away the loyalty, reliability, and obedience of the troops and functionaries of the attackers' regime. Those persons, therefore, singly and as a whole, must be given an accurate picture in order to correct the lies and to enable them to understand their role and responsibilities. The civilian defenders will need to communicate to the troops and functionaries the issues at stake in the conflict, the nature of the society that has been attacked, the perceived goals of the attackers, and the importance for the peoples of both contending parties that the attack be halted and the attempted takeover or occupation ended.

The defenders will also need to communicate that, while the defense waged against the attack will be vigorous, determined, and persistent, it will be of a special character. Its aim will be to defeat the attack and defend the society without threatening the lives and personal safety of the individuals in the attacking forces. That information and practice can be very helpful in subverting the attackers' troops and functionaries.

Such communication will lay the groundwork for later appeals. Soldiers and functionaries may be asked to be deliberately mild or inefficient in applying controls and repression, to aid the population of resisters in specific ways, to ignore orders for harsh actions, to mutiny, or to go into hiding in the countryside or among the defending population, which will help them. In such ways the attackers' capacity for repression and administration may be, under certain conditions, slowly or rapidly dissolved.

A variety of means of communication will be used to reach all these groups. The means of verbal communication may include letters, leaflets, newspapers, personal conversations, radio and television broadcasts, audio and video cassettes, wall slogans, posters, and banners. Also, drawn or painted symbols, significant colors, defiant flying of the national flag, flags at half mast, tolling of bells, silence, wailing of sirens, certain songs, and many variations on these methods may be used. All such methods should be carefully chosen to produce the kinds of effects that the defense struggle required at that stage.

Direct symbolic intervention and obstruction may also be used in communicating with the attackers' forces. For example, persons may block with their bodies—standing, sitting, or lying down—bridges, highways, streets, entrances to towns, cities, and buildings. All of these types of action primarily rely for their impact on psychological or moral influences. Mechanical obstructions may also be used. For example, people may block highways and airports with abandoned automobiles or may dismantle machinery to make facilities at seaports, airports, and railways inoperative. Although some of the mechanical obstructions may physically impede or delay the dispersion of troops or the occupation of certain locations or facilities, the effect is likely to be temporary and therefore even these obstructions have primarily psychological impact.

Another category of actions may also initially be used symbolically. These could include temporary application of such methods of noncooperation as the general strike, an economic shutdown, a massive stay-at-home (making every town and city appear empty of people), or closing all government offices. These are brief uses of some of the same methods that in sustained applications are employed in a nonviolent blitzkrieg and in long-term defensive struggles. On August 23, 1968, only a day-and-a-half after the Warsaw Pact invasion, the Czechs held a one-hour protest strike, producing an almost complete work stoppage. These short actions simply illustrate a potential. They not only communicate opposition and an intent to resist, but also demonstrate some of the more serious and substantive means of defense that lie ahead if the attack is not halted.

Defenders may also use dramatic forms of intervention in an initial strategy of communication and warning. These may include massive defiance of curfews, the holding of street parties for all (including the hostile troops), persistent conduct of "business as usual," and large-scale efforts to undermine the loyalty of the troops and minor functionaries.

These initial actions will also help to remind the attacked population of the intent to resist vigorously and firmly, of the type of resistance to be applied, and of the need to ready themselves to fulfill their responsibilities in accordance with the advance preparations and the current needs of struggle.

The attackers' countermeasures to these initial forms of communication and warning are difficult to predict. They may range from extremely mild to very brutal, even in the same situation.

The Strategy of "Nonviolent Blitzkrieg"

In this second initial strategic option, the population and institutions of the society immediately launch a major campaign of defiance and near-total noncooperation. This strategy is most likely to be used when the attackers are perceived as relatively weak and uncertain or divided in their initial decision to attack, and when the defending society views itself as strong and its defense capacity as well prepared and powerful. The aim is to convince the attackers to call off their forces quickly in the face of the massive defiance. This may take such forms as a general strike, an economic shutdown, evacuation of cities, a stay-at-home, paralyzing the political system, continuation of "business as usual," ignoring the attackers' demands, filling the streets with demonstrators or leaving them completely empty, massive attempts to subvert the attacking forces, defiant publication of newspapers, and broadcasting news of the attack and the resistance. There are many other possibilities.

Such massive defiance may also be intended to communicate to the attackers' leadership two things: that the civilian defenders are capable of waging a struggle that can deny to the attackers the fruits of victory, and that the long-term effects of the defenders' actions and influence on the morale, loyalty, and obedience of their own troops and functionaries may be potentially fatal to their reliability.

Even if a quick victory is not achieved by this strategy, at the very least, a nonviolent blitzkrieg, effectively conducted, will clearly communicate to the attackers the intent of the attacked society to defend itself. This should demonstrate in action the nature of the defense that will be used, as well as warn of future difficulties if the attackers do not withdraw. When this strategy is employed with that objective, no sharp distinction exists between the initial strategy and the subsequent defense struggle.

Civilian defenders should not assume that either of the two initial strategies of defense is likely to bring victory at that stage of the conflict. Quick success would not only require a very remarkable initial defiance by the civilian defenders, it would also need a most unusual leadership of the attacking forces (or the replacement of original leaders with ones less committed to the venture). The leadership would need to be able to admit an error or to find a way to save face while withdrawing. Only these unlikely circumstances could make a quick end of the struggle possible.

If a rapid victory does not follow the nonviolent blitzkrieg strategy, the defenders will, nevertheless, have achieved something significant: the mobilization of their forces and the communication of both their intent to resist and the special character of their defense policy. Those are similar to the results of a strategy of communication and warning. At this point it would be time to shift to another strategy, one more suited to the coming longer-term struggle and more able to counter the attackers' specific objectives.

Whatever happens in the initial stage, the defenders must be prepared to carry on the defense on the assumption that the struggle will be extended and difficult. Whether the initial action has been a campaign of communication and warning, a nonviolent blitzkrieg, or both (in combination or in one sequence or another), the initial period will at some point draw to a close. The time will come for a more sustained and substantial defense struggle.

Strategies for the Course of the Defense Struggle

In military wars the defenders may also attempt to achieve a quick, clear victory. Yet, no demoralization or sense of defeat necessarily follows their failure to do so. Instead, a shift of strategy is required for the next stages of the struggle. In civilian wars of defense this is also true. The initial campaign is to be regarded as simply the opening phase of a nonviolent struggle that, like a military campaign, may require a longer period of intense effort to achieve victory. A shift to a strategy more suitable for the next phase is, therefore, no reason for demoralization. On the contrary, the shift is a demonstration that the defenders are taking the initiative in shaping the struggle to help bring eventual victory.

With the advantage of advance planning and preparation, certain general guidelines can be established to indicate the kinds of issues and circumstances under which the population should protest and withhold cooperation, regardless of whether specific instructions have been issued by any defense organization. Then, in an emergency, such resistance would be launched even if particular leadership groups had been seized or lines of communication effectively blocked. With such guidelines, no specific directives would need to be issued. The attackers' measures would be sufficient to trigger the defense effort.

The specific issues or circumstances identified in the general guidelines for the launching of such "general resistance" might vary to some degree from society to society. They are, however, likely to include such occasions as these: the attackers' efforts to establish a substitute government or to seize control of the society's political institutions; attempts to destroy the autonomy of the society's organizations and institutions; efforts to control education, religion, and political ideas; attempts to impose censorship or suppress freedom of speech; promotion of an official ideology; and the perpetration of harsh repression and killings against any sector of the society.

With advance identification of such points and prior training of the population in the wide range of methods in civilian-based defense, the population and institutions of the society could launch such general resistance on their own initiative, with assurance that it would be within the range of good strategic judgment. Programed general resistance provides a way to utilize the vitality of spontaneous resistance while avoiding its potential damaging effects of poor focus on issues or undisciplined, counterproductive behavior.

Advance guidelines for general resistance would also make it difficult for the attackers to issue, falsely, in the name of defense leaders, counterfeit "resistance instructions" that if implemented would help to defeat the defense and would help the attackers to achieve their goals. Such instructions, obviously contradicting the standards laid out long before in defense handbooks, pamphlets, and leaflets, would then be easily identified and dismissed as provocations.

In contrast to general resistance, "organized resistance" would include those defense actions triggered by special directives from a resistance organization, and also those actions that require advance planning and group preparation. Organized resistance could be conducted as long as responsible defense leadership was able to operate and means of communication to the population at large were available. This type of resistance would have the advantage of being based on careful strategic analysis and planning, so that the specific activities would be more likely to succeed.

In facing the strategic problems of longer-range defense, the civilian defenders can apply one of two major strategies: either a massive campaign of *total noncooperation*, similar to a nonviolent blitzkrieg, or some form of *selective resistance*. The defenders may also use each of these major strategies at different times to meet special needs of the defense.

Total Noncooperation

This strategy is also called "total resistance." It involves the refusal of *all* cooperation—political, economic, and social—by the whole society against the attackers' regime and policies. It may be generally appropriate at certain stages of the defense struggle. However, total resistance is exceptionally difficult to apply in practice except for limited periods. For longer periods of time, it requires an exceptionally strong, well-prepared, and self-reliant society. The consequences of total noncooperation can be severe because of the cost of shutting down so many necessary aspects of their own society. This cost is high even if the attackers do not engage in severe repression. The defending population must be able to survive the defense struggle, which can extend over months or even years, as do most wars. Comprehensive preparations must help to make that possible, including provision of food, water, and fuel. Total noncooperation may not be used at all in certain civilian-based defense struggles because of these severe requirements.

If the strategy of total noncooperation is used in the period of substantive defense, which follows the initial period, it is likely to be applied temporarily to achieve particular purposes. The points in the struggle when this strategy may be effectively used should be carefully chosen by the defenders. This strategy should not be used for any extended period without adequate preparation. It should not be applied simply as an emotional response to the attack itself or to an especially horrific action by the opponents. This strategy might, however, be used in such situations if it is rationally selected.

Total noncooperation is probably best used at certain restricted points to achieve particular objectives within a grand strategy predominantly using selective resistance. A few examples will illustrate this. Let us suppose that the civilian defenders have for an extended period conducted selective resistance against a specific policy of the attackers. For example, the attackers may have attempted to bring the churches under effective political control. As a result of selective resistance, that measure has been seriously weakened or its implementation has been blocked, but the attackers still intend to impose the policy. In this example, the resistance by the churches and other parts of the society has proved too strong for the attackers, and they have retreated temporarily from efforts to destroy the independence of the churches. However, they still aim to resume the attack at the earliest opportunity. The strategy of total noncooperation may then be applied with the aim of forcing the attackers to abandon the policy altogether. A complete refusal of all parts of the society to have anything whatsoever to do with the attackers, their institutions, and their regulations may then be applied in an effort to force the attackers, in their weakness, to pledge publicly to recognize and respect the autonomy of religious institutions.

In case of severe brutalities against demonstrators or the general population, a short total resistance action may be appropriate to demonstrate defiance and determination. One day will usually be sufficient for that limited purpose. The action should not be extended much beyond that unless it is clear that the opponents are in a very weak position—that their troops are on the verge of mutiny, for example—or unless some other potentially decisive condition exists. Extended use of the total resistance strategy should be restricted to times when the attackers' capacity to maintain controls has been significantly weakened and when the defenders are in a very strong position to sustain total noncooperation despite possible severe repression.

This strategy may also be applied toward the end of a long struggle that has primarily consisted of various campaigns of selective resistance. The conditions for total noncooperation must obtain, however. The aim of total resistance at this point is to strike a knockout blow to defeat or disintegrate the attackers' regime, to destroy their ability to continue the venture, and to restore the society's independence and freedom.

With these exceptions, the main thrust of the society's defense must be the strategy of selective resistance.

Selective Resistance

In this strategy, the defense struggle is concentrated on certain vital social, economic, or political issues. These issues are selected because of their key role in keeping the entire social and political system out of the attackers' control. This strategy may also be called "nonviolent positional war" or "resistance at key points." Particular sections of the population would target specific issues at various times over the course of the struggle. This strategy could be targeted sequentially on several issues to keep the attackers from gaining widespread control over the society.

The strategy of selective resistance deliberately concentrates resistance on particular objectives that are especially important for the defense effort. This strategy enables the defense to be focused instead of diffused. Also, it is less exhausting. In most cases, the major responsibility for waging the defense effort will shift from one sector of the population to another as specific points and issues of resistance change.

Six major questions must be considered in selecting the points for selective resistance:

What are the attackers' main objectives?

What will prevent the attackers from gaining or maintaining control over the defenders' state apparatus or significant parts of it?

What will prevent the attackers from weakening or destroying the independence of the society's institutions and capacity for resistance?

What will concentrate defense capacity on the especially vulnerable points in the attackers' system, regime, or policies, which if broken will imperil their ability to achieve their objectives and to continue their venture?

What will enable the defenders to use their strongest qualities, capacities, and sectors of the population (and avoiding use of their weakest ones) to advance the defense?

Which specific issues typify the general principles and objectives of the struggle, issues which help to arouse a spirit of justified resistance among the defenders and make the attackers' aims and means seem the most unjustified and deserving of condemnation?

It is especially important to focus the selective resistance on points that can deny the attackers their main objectives. This is important because—as was seen in Chapter Two—the power of all rulers is dependent on sources that may be deliberately restricted or severed by the defenders' withdrawal of cooperation, assistance, and obedience.

If the attack was a coup d'état or executive usurpation, for example, then the defenders of constitutional government must make it impossible for the usurpers to consolidate control of the state apparatus and the society. The defenders could accomplish this by insisting on observance of constitutional principles, by denying authority to the usurpers, and by preventing their control of the state apparatus and the wider society. Noncooperation could be practiced by civil servants, bureaucrats, government agencies, state and local governments, police departments, and virtually all the social institutions, as well as the general population. Such methods, as seen in Chapter One, were widely practiced against the Kapp Putsch. With benefit of preparation, the impact of such measures should be significantly greater. The result would be denial of legitimacy and prevention of consolidation of effective control.

If rulers of a foreign state attacked in order to impose a government of their own choosing, then collaboration at all levels must be prevented. Would-be collaborators must be isolated, and control of the various departments, administrative bodies, police units, prison system, and military forces prevented. The defenders must also deny legitimacy to any new regime, massively refuse obedience and cooperation, and persist in their loyalty to the principles and practices of the original system.

For example, police would refuse to locate and arrest patriotic resisters. Journalists and editors would refuse to submit to censorship and would publish newspapers in defiance of prohibitions, as occurred in Poland during martial law in the 1980s. Resistance radio programs would be broadcast from hidden transmitters—as happened in Czechoslovakia in 1968. Clergymen would preach the duty to refuse help to the invaders—as both Protestant and Catholic clergy did in the Netherlands under the Nazis.

Politicians, civil servants, and judges, by ignoring or defying the enemy's illegal orders, would keep the normal machinery of government and the courts out of their control. Judicial noncooperation would become another defense weapon. Judges would declare the "officials" of the internal usurpers or foreign attackers to be without authority. They would continue to operate on the basis of the pre-invasion laws and constitution and refuse to give moral or judicial support to the invaders, even if it meant closing the courts. Civil servants and bureaucrats at times may conduct strikes, and at other times may practice a "work-on without collaboration." That is, they may persist in carrying out legally established policies, programs, and duties with indifference to, or in defiance of, contrary orders issued by the attackers.

If the invaders launched the attack to gain economic objectives, then the defenders must focus on denying these objectives. This denial can be achieved by such means as having scientists, technicians, workers, and administrators, and every institution involved, refuse cooperation and assistance. This refusal would be applied at all relevant stages, such as during the procuring of raw materials, research, planning, transportation, manufacture, supply of energy and parts, quality control, packing, and shipping. For example, workers and managers would impede exploitation of the country by selective strikes and delays—as happened in the Ruhr in 1923.

If the attackers' aim is ideological, then it is crucial to block efforts to denigrate the beliefs of the defenders' society and indoctrinate the defenders' population with the attackers' political beliefs. This can be achieved by many kinds of noncooperation by persons and institutions involved in education, religion, the media, publishing, youth activities, and government. For example, teachers would refuse to introduce propaganda into the schools (see the Norwegian example in Chapter Three). Attempts to control schools could be met with the refusal to change the school curriculum or to introduce the invaders' propaganda, while explaining to the pupils the issues at stake and continuing regular education as long as possible. If necessary, schools could be closed voluntarily and classes held in private homes. Such an extra-legal educational system operated in Nazi-occupied Poland, for example. In addition to resisting control of the educational system and the curriculum, the teachers would press the students to consider the virtues of the freedom of ideas and the importance of practicing and defending that freedom.

Selective resistance may be required to defend the society's independent institutions, the loci of power discussed in Chapter Two. The attackers may intend to establish total control over the society, eradicate the possibility of effective resistance to their new order, or restructure the whole society on a totalitarian model. The attackers may, therefore, attempt to abolish the autonomy of all existing independent institutions, to maintain them only in emasculated submissive forms, or to destroy them outright. Alternatively, the attackers may create new centrally controlled institutions that are harmonious with a totalitarian model and able to control their members. The fascist-controlled organization for Norwegian teachers, which the resistance blocked, was such a body. The defeat of that attempt, and similar ones for other professions, prevented the establishment of the corporative state in Norway. Such efforts to control the society's institutions become points for selective resistance. Defense planning and preparation should help people identify the importance of such resistance and help make the struggle successful.

Selective resistance ought also to be focused on especially vulnerable points of the attackers' regime and on the loyalty and reliability of their troops and functionaries.

The attackers cannot, of course, be expected to welcome such vigorous defense efforts, albeit nonviolent ones. They must be expected to use whatever means they believe to be effective to halt, neutralize, or crush the resistance. As discussed in Chapter Three and in this chapter, the civilian defenders must be prepared to withstand all such repression, persist in their defense, and hence bring the process of political jiujitsu into operation. Persistent defiance and a strong nonviolent discipline may make the costs of the venture unacceptable to the attackers, deny their objectives, force a halt to the attack, or even dissolve their forces and regime. As the attackers weaken and the defenders grow in strength, selective resistance campaigns of various types progressively bring the defenders closer to victory.

While some civilian-based defense struggles may be relatively brief, often the conflict may be a prolonged one. If so, the struggle is likely to be difficult. The attackers' oppression may be exceptionally harsh, involving heavy risks to the defenders and many casualties. Under the worst circumstances, many people may become discouraged and demoralized, as happened in the later months of the *Ruhrkampf*. People may also just become tired and need a rest.

Shifts in strategy, especially moving the responsibility for public action from one population group to another that is more able to act, can sometimes help. Choosing to concentrate resistance on fewer or narrower issues can also help.

In circumstances of resistance fatigue it is unlikely that there will be a widespread desire to shift to violent struggle, for it would be obvious that the chances of success by such means would be small and the number of casualties would increase. Nevertheless, it is possible that certain small groups or individuals might take desperate measures, such as planting bombs or attempting assassinations. While such acts might make the perpetrators, and even others, feel better, they would almost certainly guarantee increased repression and political losses. More importantly, such violence would likely undermine the effectiveness of nonviolent struggle. A shift to violence would require greater secrecy and hence reduce the numbers of resisters to those who could join small secret groups. It is essential that nonviolent discipline be maintained.

Even in the worst circumstances, it is crucial that resistance continue in some form. Sometimes, under certain extreme conditions, it might partially take the form of "cultural resistance." That is, people would hold on to important elements of their way of life, language, customs, beliefs, social organizations, and observances. Also, in cases when larger organizations and institutions, which had been bases for resistance, have been neutralized, controlled, or destroyed, nonviolent acts might be conducted by individuals acting alone or by extremely small, often short-lived, groups. This has been called "micro-resistance." Through all such times of great difficulty it is essential to maintain the spirit of the people, their desire to regain control of their own society, and a confidence, however shaky, that ultimately they will do so. Serious problem-solving research and strategic studies are needed on how better to deal with these extreme situations.

In time, changed circumstances, unexpected events, new resistance initiatives, and renewed spirits and energies can lead to increased defense activities and the generation of greater capacity to pursue the struggle. At the very times when a struggle is most difficult, significant changes favoring the nonviolent resisters may be developing unseen. These include the appearance or heightening of doubts, disagreements, and objections in the attackers' own camp.

Whether an exceptionally difficult period occurs or not, as the defenders' strength increases, changes of strategy may be required. For example, instead of concentrating primarily on limited campaigns of selective resistance, there may be opportunities to conduct increasingly widespread resistance. In favorable circumstances it may even be possible to move toward total noncooperation to strike a knockout blow. On other occasions, different end-game strategies may be required. In any case, it will be important to develop specific steps to bring the defense struggle to a successful conclusion.

International Support for Civilian-based Defense

Countries with civilian-based defense policies can participate in a great variety of international activities on bilateral, multilateral, regional, and world bases. These countries need not be isolationist simply because they lack military capacities—unless they chose to be. Many of their international activities would have little directly to do with deterrence and defense needs; some activities would be intended to alleviate pressing needs, resolve issues underlying conflicts, correct unfounded suspicions and misunderstandings, and improve mutual understanding and friendship. These activities could reduce the number and intensity of future international conflicts.

Some of the international cooperation and assistance of these countries will focus directly on the preparations for and conduct of civilian-based defense. The nature of this defense policy makes it unnecessary to be as secretive as one usually is in military defense matters. This makes possible widespread sharing of knowledge and know-how among countries already implementing the policy and countries investigating it. Such countries could with mutual benefit share research results, policy analyses, plans for preparation and training, and knowledge about potential attackers. They can share information about strategies for resisting particular types of attack, means to maximize defense effectiveness, methods of maintaining resistance in the face of repression, and measures to meet the society's material needs when under attack.

Basic studies and contingency planning in these areas and in preparation and training could be initially conducted by individual countries, private institutions, several countries or treaty partners working cooperatively, by regional organizations, or United Nations agencies. These same bodies could also, by treaty arrangements or in response to particular crises, provide nonmilitary assistance to countries with civilian-based defense policies facing attack.

Appropriate types of assistance include (1) access to printing and broadcasting facilities for the attacked country; (2) provision of food and medical supplies; (3) transmission to the outside world of news about the defense struggle and the aggressors' actions; (4) mobilization of international economic and diplomatic sanctions against the attackers; and (5) communication to the attackers' troops, functionaries, and population of information about the attack (such as the issues at stake, forms of resistance and repression being used, news of dissent among the attackers' usual supporters, and reports of pleas for help in ending the attack and in restoring international friendship and cooperation).

All such international assistance is extremely important, but the main burden of the defense must be borne by the population of the attacked society itself. No substitute exists for self-reliance, sound preparation, and genuine strength in civilian-based defense.

Success and Failure

The difficulties that the attackers will encounter when confronted by a well-prepared, sophisticated civilian-based defense must not be underestimated. The defenders' capacity to mobilize their own power of resistance and to undermine, directly and indirectly, the sources of the attackers' power can produce dramatic changes in power relationships. Given real internal strength, strategic and tactical wisdom, discipline and persistence in the face of repression, and the capacity to strike at the opponents' weaknesses, the civilian defenders should be able to frustrate and finally defeat their adversary.

The very terms *success* and *failure* must be used with precise meanings in discussions of this policy. This is necessary both to evaluate the effectiveness of any given application of civilian-based defense and to compare this policy with military defense.

Success in civilian-based defense is measured by whether the defenders have actually achieved their goals, that is, to dissolve the attack and restore their independent capacity to live by their own principles and institutions.

Failure in civilian-based defense, on the other hand, means that the attackers have gained their objectives.

As with military struggles, not every attempt to apply civilian-based defense will succeed. This type of struggle, like any other, can be successful only if its requirements for effectiveness are met, as discussed in Chapter Three. Military defeat is likely to result from vast physical destruction, loss of life, demoralization, and a perceived inability to bring the struggle to a successful conclusion. These conditions can also accompany failure in civilian-based defense, but they need not.

Instead, there may be times when one side temporarily gains or loses strength and achieves only some of its immediate objectives. The civilian defenders may be required to endure difficult times of great suffering and many casualties. As long as they maintain their will for defense, however, they can strengthen themselves and their institutions and refine their ability to wage nonviolent struggle. The defenders can increase their courage and persist in the face of intimidation and repression and apply new strategies to create conditions more favorable to the cause.

Even apparent defeat is not permanent. Although the defenders may not have achieved their goals at any given time, it is possible that they may do so at a later point. To the degree that the spirit of resistance and the resilience of the society's independent institutions are maintained, the population can renew the defense struggle at another time. In the interim, rest, renewal of the society's strength and its capacity to rebound from attacks, the development of new strategies, and the selection of new, initially limited, and achievable goals may be necessary. Success with these can lead to adoption of strategies with more ambitious objectives. In other words, definitive defeat in civilian-based defense need never exist as long as the population and society survive. The case of improvised nonviolent struggle in Czechoslovakia provides an example of this. The 1968–1969 Warsaw Pact invasion and subsequent collapse of the Dubček leadership was followed by a harsh period under the Husak regime. Advocates of freedom suffered disgrace and imprisonment, such as members of Charter 77. However, in late 1989, the popular nonviolent movement was renewed, this time forcing the collapse of Communist rule and the restoration of political rights in Czechoslovakia.

During nonviolent struggles there are likely to be considerable periods when the defenders have been partially successful but also have suffered some setbacks. At these times, it is very important that they fully recognize their achievements and strengths. As has sometimes happened in past nonviolent struggles, people have fought well and made significant gains but, because they had not yet achieved their full objectives, have thought that they had been defeated. They have therefore lost spirit and allowed their resistance to wither or collapse. In effect, they capitulated, thereby defeating themselves. That must be avoided in civilian-based defense.

In the midst of an on-going struggle, the civilian defenders can assess how successful they have been to that point by addressing the following questions:

To what degree have the civilian *defenders* maintained, weakened, or strengthened their will to resist?

To what degree have the various persons and groups among the *attackers* maintained, weakened, or strengthened their will to continue the attack and to pursue the original goals?

To what degree have the *independent institutions* (loci of power) of the defending society maintained, lost, or augmented their capacity to struggle and to deny to the attackers the needed sources of power?

To what degree have the *defenders* and the *attackers*, respectively, demonstrated good strategic judgment or ineptness, and have their strategic judgments deteriorated or improved?

To what degree have the civilian *defenders* increased their ability to wage noncooperation and defiance, their capacity for disciplined action, and their ability to fulfill the requirements for effectiveness in nonviolent struggle?

To what degree have the *attackers' population, agents of repression, and administrators* experienced high morale, support for the attack, and active assistance to it, or instead experienced poor morale, dissent, unreliability, or opposition to the attack?

To what degree, respectively, have the *attackers' and the defenders' international friends and needed economic or political partners* continued their prior relationships, offered support, or disapproved of their actions and withdrawn cooperation?

To what degree have the *defenders* maintained their capacity for autonomy and ability to meet their economic needs?

To what degree have the *attackers' measures of manipulation and repression* succeeded or been ineffective in halting the defense and gaining the attackers' objectives? Or have they actually increased the defenders' resistance, aroused opposition in the attackers' own camp, and provoked international action?

To what degree have the *defenders* continued or even increased their resistance in the face of repression and brutalities?

To what degree have the *attackers' original objectives* (economic, political, ideological, or other) been attained?

Which side is exercising the initiative in the conflict?

When the answers to these questions indicate that the defenders have made some gains but have also experienced some losses, it is time for them to take corrective action to increase their chances of success. They then need to take the following steps: increase their personal strength; maintain and expand their societal strength; identify and apply their most relevant and effective leverages on the attackers; improve their strategic judgment; focus resistance on the attackers' weak points; and act with deliberation, courage, and steadfastness.

The criteria for evaluating the final results of a civilian-based defense struggle go beyond determining whether the attackers have been physically destroyed or have capitulated to superior military forces. Whether a particular civilian-based defense struggle has been successful would be determined by answers to questions such as these:

Have the *defenders* continued to deny the legitimacy of the aggressors' regime and to maintain belief in their own principles and in the right to choose their own system and policies?

Have the *defenders* maintained the autonomy of their society and met its needs, despite an occupation or a usurping regime?

Have the *attackers* achieved or been denied their objectives (economic, political, ideological, or other), and to what degrees?

Have the *attackers* gained or lost important international support?

Has the *attackers' will to prosecute the attack* been maintained or changed?

Have the *defenders* blocked the establishment and consolidation of a substitute government of any type?

Have the *attackers' forces* withdrawn or disintegrated?

Are the *attackers* likely to launch similar ventures in the future?

Has the *aggressors' regime* survived or been replaced?

Not all civilian-based defense struggles will end with clear success or failure measured by these standards. Rather, as shown in Chapter Three, at times there may be degrees of success and failure.

The most important single factor in achieving success by civilian-based defense is that the attacked society is able to maintain its self-direction and autonomy even with the presence of ruthless would-be rulers backed by hostile troops. This capacity hinges on the strength and determination of the populace and the society's groups and institutions (the loci of power discussed in Chapters Two and Three).

The strength to block the attackers' objectives may take a variety of forms. The following are only a few examples: the attackers' attempts to gain legitimacy for a new regime are blocked and the populace remains loyal to the pre-attack constitutional system; the effort to impose a new government fails, as it is impossible simply to harness the previous bureaucracy and agencies of enforcement; government bodies continue to apply the legitimate policies and laws and refuse to implement the attackers' substitutes; the society as a whole isolates and ignores any new bureaucracy or agencies created by the attackers; a de facto free press continues to operate despite the attackers' censorship and prohibitions; radio and television broadcasts supporting the resistance continue from hidden transmitters or from the territory of sympathetic neighboring countries; attempts to control religious organizations meet massive defiance by the religious bodies and the population of believers; attempts to ban all political opposition are met with increased political interest and activities among the population, with a multiplication of active political groups; attempts to replace independent professional organizations and unions result in their invigorated persistence, thus becoming stronger organs of resistance; other social organizations, ranging from gardening societies to sports clubs, become politically relevant centers of communication and activity loyal to the principles of the society; efforts to harness the economy to serve new masters are counterproductive, as strikes, boycotts, deliberate inefficiencies, and slow-downs reduce both quantity and quality of products and simultaneously increase the costs of attempting to make the economy work for the attackers, far beyond any gains they may receive. Such examples could be multiplied several times over.

In short, the civilian defenders prove able to block the establishment of controls over the society, to prevent an effective collaborationist or substitute government, to defeat the attackers' political, economic, ideological, or other goals, while increasing the economic and political costs of the attackers' attempts beyond any acceptable level.

Under some circumstances—not always—the attackers may find that their own troops and functionaries become more and more disenchanted with the venture and their personal roles in it. Collaborators who have helped the attackers in the past may have second thoughts, become unreliable, and even join the resistance as the situation changes and they become targets of special "decollaboration" activities by the resisters. Even the attackers' home population gradually may begin to dissent and to oppose the venture. Members of the international community may increasingly condemn the attack, then shift from vocal condemnation to international action, perhaps including economic, political, and diplomatic sanctions.

When some combination of these developments occurs, the attack will have been dissolved, and the attacked society's independence and chosen way of life restored.

Notes

This chapter draws heavily on Gene Sharp, "Civilian-based Defense: A New Deterrence and Defense Policy." The article was originally commissioned for UNESCO and later published in Yoshikazu Sakamoto, editor, *Strategic Doctrines and Their Alternatives* (New York: Gordon and Breach, 1987), pp. 227–262. A related discussion of these strategic principles in a Western European context is contained in Gene Sharp, *Making Europe Unconquerable* (London: Taylor & Francis, 1985, and Cambridge, Mass.: Ballinger, 1985; second American edition, with a foreword by George Kennan, Cambridge, Mass.: Ballinger, 1986).

For a discussion related to "forward defense," see Sharp, *Making Europe Unconquerable* (second American edition), pp. 60–61.

For further discussion of the problems of employing sabotage within a nonviolent movement, see Gene Sharp, *The Politics of Nonviolent Action* (Boston: Porter Sargent, 1973), pp. 608–611.

For a discussion of the role of the radio in resistance movements, see H. Gordon Skilling, *Czechoslovakia's Interrupted Revolution* (Princeton, N.J.: Princeton University Press, 1976), pp. 777–778. See also Joseph Wechsberg, *The Voices* (Garden City, N.Y.: Doubleday, 1969).

On the protest strike in Czechoslovakia, see Skilling, *Czechoslovakia's Interrupted Revolution*, p. 775.

The quotations on changes in Nazi policies against the population in the occupied Soviet Union are from Alexander Dallin, *German Rule in Russia, 1941–1945: A Study of Occupation Policies* (New York: St. Martin's Press, 1957, and London: Macmillan, 1957), pp. 218, 497, and 550. Nazi attitudes and intentions toward the Eastern Europeans are also discussed.

For an introductory essay on the Holocaust experience, see Gene Sharp, "The Lesson of Eichmann. A Review-Essay on Hannah Arendt's *Eichmann in Jerusalem*," in *Social Power and Political Freedom* (Boston: Porter Sargent, 1980). For relevant studies of genocide, see, among others: Gerald Reitlinger, *The Final Solution: The Attempt to Exterminate the Jews of Europe 1939–1945* (New York: A. S. Barnes, 1961); Raul Hilberg, *The Destruction of the European Jews* (Chicago: Quadrangle Books, and London: W. H. Allen, 1961, and revised edition, New York: Holmes and Meier, 1985); Nora Levin, *The Holocaust: The Destruction of European Jewry 1933–1945* (New York: Schocken Books, 1973); Helen Fein, *Accounting for Genocide* (New York: Free Press, and London: Macmillan, 1979).

The term "nonviolent Blitzkrieg" was introduced by Theodor Ebert.

The discussion of the distinction between "general resistance" and "organized resistance" was stimulated by Lars Porsholt. See Lars Porsholt, "On the Conduct of Civilian Defence," in T. K. Mahadevan, Adam Roberts, and Gene Sharp, editors, *Civilian Defence: An Introduction* (New Delhi: Gandhi Peace Foundation, and Bombay: Bharatiya Vidya Bhavan, 1967), pp. 145–149.

The term "micro-resistance" was introduced by Professor Arne Næss. See Arne Næss, "Non-military Defence and Foreign Policy," in Adam Roberts, Jerome Frank, Arne Næss, and Gene Sharp, *Civilian Defence* (London: Peace News, 1964), p. 42.

Five _____

Toward Transarmament

Improvised Nonviolent Struggle and Civilian-based Defense

CIVILIAN-BASED DEFENSE is being developed as a policy for research, consideration, and adoption *in advance* of defense crises. This policy requires preparation and training of the population for its use. However, defense crises are likely to occur for countries that have not already adopted this policy. When surrender and submission to aggression are unacceptable, and military responses are obviously futile or suicidal, cases of *improvised* nonviolent struggle against coups and invasions will, in all probability, continue.

Despite the lack of advance preparation, future struggles are likely to be more sophisticated than those outlined in Chapter One. The reasons for this are twofold: general knowledge about the workings of nonviolent action and civilian-based defense is spreading rapidly and a growing number of countries have had direct experience with the use of nonviolent struggle for diverse purposes.

Improvised nonviolent struggle for defense is not, however, civilian-based defense. In most cases, improvised nonviolent resistance will be significantly weaker than a well-prepared civilian-based defense policy, for it will lack the advantages of preparation and planning. For example, without preparation there would be no deterrent effect, which might prevent an attack in the first place. Also, the skills, training, strategic acumen, and resources that can be gained during years of planning and preparation would all be missing in an improvised struggle.

Planning and preparation, consequently, make nonviolent struggle for defense substantially more effective (as is similarly true in military efforts). The results of preparation are likely to include the following: development of a deterrence and dissuasion effect; strategic assessment and planning; attitudinal preparation (to prevent confusion, fear, and uncertainty); training by the society's institutions, civil servants, police, remaining military forces, and governmental bodies for conducting noncooperation and defiance in case of attack; formulation of contingency plans; stockpiling of equipment, food, water, means of energy, communication, and other resources; and establishment of organizations of specialists in civilian-based defense strategy.

In combination with planning and preparation, dissemination of both general publications (and other means of communications such as cassettes and videos) and specific pamphlets and handbooks (as affecting transportation, the media, schools, religious bodies, labor, business, and the like) would help spread knowledge of how to operate effective civilian-based defense. This would make it possible for the struggle to continue within the requirements for nonviolent struggle and the defined strategic plans, even though some of the earlier, more visible, leadership might have been arrested or killed.

The advantages of advance preparations provide good reasons for countries which might face a defense crisis to consider adopting a civilian-based defense, either as a supplementary component of predominantly military policies or as their basic deterrence and defense policy.

Motives for Waging Civilian-based Defense

In most cases, the motives for implementing civilian-based defense would be the same as those of people who have fought in wars and who now support military warfare for defense. People fight to defend their country because they love it, cherish its independence, and want to preserve their way of life (although they may also wish to improve their society). People are likely to fight because they believe it is their moral, patriotic, or religious duty. While people may be quite happy to argue among themselves about politics, social policy, and even basic principles, they are likely to unite in the conviction that no foreign government or internal clique of would-be dictators shall be permitted to rule them.

All these are powerful motives for participating in civilian-based defense. As in military wars, these social and political motives often combine with personal, individual ones. These may include the desire to make a difference with one's life, to become important, to help defend one's family and friends, and to prove one's bravery, initiative, and willingness to sacrifice for others. Also, the minority section of the population, which for personal, religious, or ethical reasons has not supported, or objected to, violent measures will likely be able to participate fully in civilian-based defense. Additionally, in civilian-based defense all age groups and both sexes are able to participate in the various aspects of the nonviolent struggle. Their motives and willingness to participate can be fulfilled because the nature of the defense permits all of them to play significant roles.

For everyone in the population, however, a primary reason for support of and participation in this defense policy will be recognition of the capacity and power of civilian-based defense to fight aggression and internal takeovers. This recognition will help inspire the population as a whole to wage the defense struggle with spirit, determination, and tenacity.

Are Fundamental Changes Necessary Preconditions for Civilian-based Defense?

Various intellectuals have at times argued that mass nonviolent struggle is impossible for any of a whole series of impressive-sounding reasons. These have included genetics, child-rearing practices, the culture, the distorting effects of the social system, the type of educational system, family patterns and sex roles, accepted religious doctrines, or the political system in control.

All of those "reasons" for the impossibility of mass nonviolent struggle—and therefore of a civilian-based defense policy—can be discarded for purposes of this discussion: mass nonviolent struggle exists and is therefore possible. Some of the given "reasons" are associated with proposals to improve human society and individual lives. The merits of such proposals should be considered separately and not confused with the requirements of nonviolent struggle and a civilian-based defense policy.

Some intellectuals still argue, however, that fundamental changes in human beings or the world are required before a civilian-based defense policy becomes realistic. Occasionally, though much less often than in the past, someone who has not carefully studied civilian-based defense will say in effect, "Well, that is all very fine in an ideal world, and when it comes into existence I will support that kind of defense."

These friendly commentators often mean that before civilian-based defense can be realistic one of three fundamental changes must have occurred: (1) "human nature" has been changed so that people are more loving and cooperative, (2) the international situation has been so transformed that military systems have disappeared, or (3) the social system has undergone a major transformation producing greater social justice and equality (presumably removing the "causes" of wars). While it might be highly desirable to achieve such changes (however unlikely they may be), none of them is a prerequisite for implementing civilian-based defense. To the contrary, we know that nonviolent struggle has operated in the "real world" for centuries, if not millennia. We know also that this technique has already been improvised for defense against hostile attacks. However, let us look more closely at three of the arguments that a fundamental change in people or society is required before civilian-based defense becomes realistic.

Is a Change of "Human Nature" Required?

Sociologists, anthropologists, psychologists, philosophers, and theologians—as well as all the rest of us—differ about what "human nature" is, and what we might prefer it to be. However, those fascinating (or boring) discussions are all irrelevant. No change in the nature of human beings is required for masses of people to use nonviolent struggle.

The fact is that, contrary to popular misperceptions, nonviolent struggle has occurred very widely throughout human history and has been waged by human beings at least as imperfect as we are today. The ability to resist without violence is *not* necessarily rooted in altruism, forgiveness, belief in love, turning the other cheek, or a desire for "self-suffering" to remove evil.

Instead, nonviolent struggle is rooted in a human propensity—evidenced also in many domesticated animals (including not only the mule but our pet dogs and cats)—to be stubborn, to persist in doing what has been forbidden, and to refuse to do what has been ordered. This stubborn streak can be easily observed in children today. (We might just remember that we did many such acts when we were young—or perhaps still do!) Fortunately, we are also capable of working together and even being altruistic; but human stubbornness is very widespread and is often a valuable component of our personalities. It is the most fundamental psychological basis of nonviolent resistance. Nonviolent struggle is simply the collective application of human stubbornness for social, economic, or political objectives.

A Change in the International System?

Nor does changing over from military to civilian-based defense require any prior transformation of the international system, the disappearance of military threats, or universal adoption of the policy. External threats to the security of numerous nations are likely to continue in the foreseeable future. Conflicts over natural resources, regional political influence, ideologies, geography, socio-economic models of development, and the like are not about to disappear from the international scene. That reality is among the reasons for the development and consideration of a civilian-based defense policy. All societies should have a capacity to deter and defeat attacks in a conflict-filled world by means that do not themselves threaten the population with either years of paramilitary conflict or quick, massive annihilation.

Civilian-based defense seeks to deal with that reality: it is designed to *strengthen* the society's actual deterrence and defense capacity.

Therefore, there is no reason to wait to adopt it until potential enemies have done so, any more than governments have waited to adopt new, more powerful military weapons until their enemies have first procured them. A basic change from the military "weapons system" to the armory of civilian-based defense will only occur when the new, nonviolent weapons are perceived as being at least as powerful as the old ones.

A Change in the Social System?

Certain advocates, as well as critics, of civilian-based defense have argued that the adoption and effective implementation of this policy would require the *prior* transformation of the social system toward significantly greater democracy, equality, and decentralization of power. They have argued—usually from certain ethical principles or ideological perspectives (such as socialist, anarchist, or pacifist)—that only a "just society" or a "nonviolent society" can be defended by nonviolent means. Almost never do these critics cite historical evidence to support their arguments.

As the examples in Chapter One show, improvised nonviolent struggle has in fact been used with a moderate degree of success to defend "imperfect" societies from internal and external attack. These societies sometimes contained social injustices, class rule, ethnic or linguistic heterogeneity, and even extreme internal conflicts. This was demonstrated in Germany in the 1920s. The Weimar Republic was hardly a socially harmonious society, yet it officially used improvised noncooperation and nonviolent defiance against both the 1920 Kapp Putsch and the 1923 Franco-Belgian invasion and occupation. The repeated occurrence of nonviolent struggle in many parts of the world under highly adverse circumstances, and at times against foreign aggressors, military cliques, and internal dictatorships, is evidence that the deliberate use of this type of defense is possible in the future.

Although social harmony, greater social justice, and a vibrant democracy would be more conducive to the use and success of a civilian-based defense policy, these conditions are not prerequisites. Civilian-based defense does not require ideal social conditions for its adoption and practice.

Some social radicals may grant that civilian-based defense is possible, but argue that defending the existing social order by any means is undesirable. These people and groups may be so dissatisfied with the existing society, its violation of certain ideals, its injustices and various types of oppression, that they will chafe at the idea that they should defend the government and system they have previously condemned.

Their aim has been not to preserve that system, but to transform or replace it, so as to achieve greater political freedom, a more vigorous democracy, or a more just social and economic system. There are, however, good reasons for even these radical critics to support a civilian-based defense policy.

When the society is attacked by those who want to impose a domestic or foreign dictatorship, it is the responsibility and opportunity of even the most radical advocates of social change to rally to the defense of the attacked, imperfect society. *A prerequisite to making a society better is to prevent it from being made worse.*

After a successful civilian-based defense, there will be opportunities for the advocates of change to gain support for their proposals. The populace of that country, having experienced its own power, would be in a stronger position to achieve internal social change nonviolently. Radical groups may also have gained increased credibility through their vigorous participation in the civilian struggle against the attackers, as opposed to having tried to use the situation only to advance their own partisan advantages, as certain political groups have done in the past.

While highly imperfect societies have been defended by improvised nonviolent struggle, this does not mean that the social and political conditions are irrelevant to the effectiveness of civilian-based defense. There is a relation between the nature of the society to be defended and the capacity of civilian-based defense to do so. This is for two reasons. First, the intensity of popular will to defend the society and the number of potential collaborators may be highly influenced by the degree to which people are satisfied with the existing social order. Second, diffusion of power throughout the institutions of the society (the loci of power) would increase the resilience of the society and its defense capacity. Therefore, an important part of the long-term preparation for civilian-based defense would be to improve the quality of democracy and justice in the society.

Certain military specialists (such as the late Oxford military historian Professor Norman Gibbs and the late Hon. Alastair Buchan, who founded the Institute for Strategic Studies in London) were of the opinion that preparations for civilian-based defense would require the society to take steps to decentralize power within the normal peacetime society. They had no objections to this, and saw such measures to have independent merit, but argued that such social and political corollaries to adoption of the policy should be acknowledged.

Even when steps to remove injustices and to diffuse power in the society are not taken, effective nonviolent struggle may still be possible. This can occur if the attacked population experiences an outpouring of patriotism and a widespread conviction that the attackers must be defeated so that the domestic problems can be dealt with at a later date. Indeed, the civilian defense struggle may help the population to gain the needed self-confidence and self-reliance to advance the democratization of the society after the defense crisis.

This does not mean, however, that *every* political system can be successfully defended by nonviolent struggle. The most clear negative case is that of extreme dictatorships. These are regimes whose brutalities have aroused severe hatred among the population and which have severely restricted or abolished the independent institutions of a society that could serve as loci of power for mobilizing and conducting civilian-based defense. Such regimes are unlikely to find among their populace either the will or the capacity for such defense struggles.

However, even people living under highly oppressive regimes might wage improvised nonviolent struggle against foreign attackers. If the populace had a sufficient distaste for the aggressors, the people could mobilize themselves to defend their right of self-determination. An invasion of a society ruled by an authoritarian system might thereby arouse an enthusiastic and effective improvised nonviolent defense struggle on behalf of the country as distinct from the government. In the process of struggle they might create new independent institutions, which simultaneously would be organs for defending and reshaping the previous political system. This popular mobilization could then lead to increased participation in political life, the building of additional autonomous institutions, and a significant modification or replacement of the earlier system.

Alternatively, officials of a highly centralized society could deliberately move toward decentralization and democracy (as developments in the Soviet Union under Gorbachev and in Spain under the successors to Franco show). Such a reform regime, if genuinely committed to basic change, could even contemplate introducing elements of a civilian-based defense policy. That government could then act on its own initiative, perhaps with the stimulus or support of a dissatisfied public, to resolve popular grievances, decentralize institutions, increase popular political participation in decision making, and develop a popular desire and ability to defend the society and its growing freedoms by civilian struggle. This could be especially important in blocking a possible coup d'état by hard-liners among the ruling party, the political police, and the military forces.

Except where clearly noted, it is assumed in the remainder of the book that we are discussing consideration of civilian-based defense within a political system that has reasonable claims to being called a democracy.

A Transpartisan Approach to Consideration of the Policy

If the substance of a possible civilian-based defense policy is presented on the basis of its potential utility—without ideological baggage—such a policy might well receive widespread support across the political spectrum in a democratic society. To make fair consideration of the policy on its merits possible, it is highly important that the presentation and evaluation of civilian-based defense proposals be made in a "transpartisan" manner. The policy must *not* be tied to any particular political or ideological group or perspective. Individual countries, political groups, and the like, could, however, reasonably argue that the policy was fully compatible with, and even required by, their own ideals or ideology, but they ought not to claim that it belongs exclusively to them. In general, civilian-based defense would be best presented in ways that make it sensible and appealing to groups and individuals holding a great variety of political views and differing attitudes toward military means and past wars.

Very importantly, no peace or pacifist group or radical political organization should identify itself as the prime advocate of civilian-based defense. Neither should the new policy be presented in ways that might alienate conservatives and members of the existing defense establishment or the independent social groups and institutions that would bear responsibility for carrying out the future policy.

All sectors of the society ought to play important roles not only in exploring and evaluating civilian-based defense, but also in preparing for and implementing the policy. Indeed, it is imperative that many sectors of the society participate in the adoption of this policy. A civilian-based defense must rest on broad national consensus because it must be implemented by the general population and institutions of the society, not special forces alone. Such consensus and solidarity cannot be built upon purely partisan approaches. Staunch critics of a society's present defense policy must join with fervent supporters of that policy to open a rigorous investigation and discussion of the new civilian-based defense proposals.

A transpartisan approach would not erase or ignore important political differences within the society. Rather, it would aim at incorporating people holding various perspectives in support of the development and adoption of civilian-based defense. Assume, for example, that the immediate policy proposal is to integrate only a small civilian-based component into the society's existing, predominantly military, defense preparations. Groups advocating full adoption of civilian-based defense should support the limited component on the grounds that as more is learned, public confidence in civilian-based defense would likely grow, making total changeover to this policy at some point a serious political possibility. On the other hand, present supporters of the existing military policies could sincerely support the incorporation of the small civilian-based component, since it would add an extra layer of deterrence and defense to the existing military posture. Some of these people might also hope, and expect, that acceptance of that small civilian-based component would be the end of the matter!

A future decision on whether to expand the initially small civilian-based defense component, or eventually to move toward full adoption, could then be based in part on the merits revealed by an *existing* civilian-based defense component and by the subsequent research and policy studies of its capacities. Expansion of the civilian-based defense component could then become more sensible in the minds of most people: the once unthinkable may gradually become the obvious and realistic choice.

The ultimate decision on rejecting, retaining, or fully adopting this policy would be determined by the degree to which civilian-based defense is deemed to be adequate to deter and defend against internal coups and foreign aggression. *This book is based on the assumption that no country will permanently relinquish its military options unless and until it has a deserved confidence in a viable, developed civilian-based defense policy.*

In most situations, the adoption of a new defense posture could hardly be achieved without the participation of the society's existing defense establishment. Preliminary evidence from the addition of non-violent resistance components into the defense policies of Sweden, Austria, Switzerland, and Yugoslavia indicate that the participation of the defense ministries in the consideration and development of civilian-based defense is both possible and constructive. Military institutions and personnel have also been involved in serious examinations of this policy in Norway, Finland, and several other countries.

There might be exceptions to the involvement of the military in the consideration and adoption of civilian-based defense: a newly independent country may lack military forces, a country may have been permanently demilitarized by international agreement, or the geopolitical situation and military realities might exclude the building of effective military capacity. Another exception might exist in cases where the military forces have acted primarily as agents for imposing dictatorships on the population. In certain revolutionary situations, such military organizations may have been soundly defeated and disbanded. In virtually all other situations, however, a "transpartisan" approach is required. This approach needs to cut across traditional partisan barriers and political alignments. It also needs to involve the society's various political parties, traditional military defense institutions, and non-governmental organizations—in short, all of the society's state and non-state institutions and the general population.

The Process of Transarmament

The process of changing over from military-based defense to civilian-based defense is called "transarmament." This is *not* "disarmament," if that term is understood as the reduction or abandonment of defense capacity. Instead, transarmament is the process of changing the type of "armament" from one relying on military forces and weaponry to one depending on the whole population using the psychological, social, economic, and political weapons outlined in Chapter Three.

This discussion assumes that transarmament will proceed in accordance with democratically made decisions in which the government plays a major role in both the choice of civilian-based defense and its preparations. This need not be a universal pattern, however, and governmental plans made without the support and participation of the society are unlikely to be sound or to be implemented effectively.

In some cases, especially when the government's democratic qualities are limited, societal groups and institutions may proceed with preparations for civilian-based defense prior to or parallel with governmental evaluation and decision making. The recommendations of non-state institutions, including occupational and professional groups, might be examined to determine whether they could be integrated into a comprehensive plan to serve as the basis for a government-adopted policy. In most cases, however, governmental initiatives are more likely to precede consideration by the non-state institutions and to provide the general framework for developing more specific plans.

Obviously, the process, occasion, extent, and timing of transarmament will vary widely from one situation to another. These will depend to a significant degree on the circumstances and capacities of present policies. Most important, however, will be the degree of understanding of civilian-based defense and the assessment of its capacity to deter and successfully defend against potential attackers.

In most cases, civilian-based defense could not be adopted quickly as a full substitute for military defense. Given the complexity of transforming an entire nations' system of defense, and the relatively untested nature of a civilian-based defense policy, rapid replacement of military defenses is virtually impossible. Some of the arguments that an abrupt abandonment of military systems is possible have been derived from false premises. These include the notion that such a shift could be accomplished by mass conversion to pacifism, or that

the shift would "naturally" follow from the use of nonviolent resistance for other purposes, or that a social revolution would eliminate the need for the military. However, there is no historical evidence
that a shift to nonviolent struggle in defense is at all likely to occur
on the basis of massive individual conversions to religious nonviolence. Nor will a shift to civilian-based defense happen as a natural consequence of the use of nonviolent resistance to achieve liberation from foreign rule or an internal dictatorship, as experience from
India, Iran, and elsewhere shows. Neither does a civilian-based defense policy come into existence simply as a result of a revolution
that aims to establish a new social order in which class oppression
and exploitation—presumed causes of military systems—would not
exist, as evidence from Russia, China, Cuba, Vietnam, and Nicaragua
demonstrates.

Rapid changeovers are undesirable in most situations because quick
shifts to civilian-based defense could not be well planned. That could
be fatal. Without adequate, comprehensive, and competent preparation, the civilian-based defense policy, when put to the test, probably
would be little more effective than improvised nonviolent resistance.
The resulting ill-prepared defense efforts would be especially subject to
weaknesses and possible defeat. Ill-prepared, incompetent, and ineffective resistance practiced under the name of civilian-based defense
could well discredit the whole policy.

Civilian-based defense is likely to be adopted more or less on the
same basis that innovations in military policies are accepted. The new
conceptions and weapons systems must be seen as improvements on
past defense assumptions, plans, and weaponry. Most countries interested in this policy will adopt a gradual, incremental approach, slowly
incorporating and testing civilian-based defense components in their
overall, predominantly military, defense postures. These components
may be intended to provide policy options for special contingencies or
to provide a complementary defense capacity for tasks not otherwise
covered.

In this incremental approach to transarmament, the preparation and
training would begin on a relatively modest basis, while the existing
military policy is still in place. The civilian-based component could
then be expanded in stages. The military capacity would not be down-
graded or eliminated at first. There are two reasons for this. First, the
population would be unwilling to reduce its military preparations until
viable substitute civilian-based defense options were in place. Second,
even given the will for change, the transition from a military policy to
a civilian policy would require considerable time, as previously noted.
Preparations, training of the population, and other adjustments (in

some cases including economic conversion) would need to be developed and implemented.

The emphasis in transarmament is primarily on the *increase in effective defense capacity* through development of the new civilian-based policy, *not* on the reduction or abandonment of military weaponry. That would *follow* the development of deserved confidence in the new nonviolent deterrence and defense system. Gradually, if confidence in the deterrence and defense capacities of the expanding new policy spreads, the existing military weaponry would likely be seen as less and less necessary. This would be especially the case toward the end of the transarmament process. At that point, the military hardware could be gradually reduced and abandoned as antiquated weapons, as were bows and arrows.

In all countries not subject to imminent attack, time is available for reasoned evaluation and decision as to whether to change defense policies. This chapter is based on the assumption that there is time to consider civilian-based defense, to research its capacities, dynamics, requirements, and strategic principles.

The steps in the incremental adoption of civilian-based defense will be of varying substance and duration. There is no blueprint of steps and time scale that is applicable to all countries and situations. Careful and unique plans would be required for each. In general, however, the following elements will be included in the process of consideration and adoption:

research;
public education;
policy and feasibility studies;
evaluation by the public, private organizations, official institutions, defense departments and ministries, and legislatures;
introduction of a modest civilian-based component (perhaps for specific purposes);
preparing and training of the populace;
consideration of adding other purposes for the use of civilian-based defense;
consideration of the desirability and viability of retaining both military and civilian-based components or shifting further, or fully, to civilian-based defense;
legislative and administrative action on these decisions;
strengthening the capacities of civilian-based defense; and
unification of the defense policy.

Major attention must be given to comparative analyses of the advantages and disadvantages, the capacities and incapacities, of military-based and civilian-based defenses to meet security needs for the present and the foreseeable future. This will be true both in the initial stage, when the society first decides to start civilian-based defense preparations, and also in the later stage, when it is determining whether the new policy will be adequate on its own. In an assessment of the relevance of civilian-based defense to the security needs of a specific country, the following factors become crucial:

- the nature and circumstances of the country's external situation and security threats;
- the nature and circumstances of the country's internal situation and danger of usurpations;
- the country's perceived options in deterrence and defense; and
- the assessment and perception of the viability of civilian-based defense to meet those defense needs.

Models of Policy Consideration and Transarmament

No single model of policy consideration and partial or full transarmament can be created that will be applicable to all countries and situations. It is, however, possible to conceive of several general models by which civilian-based defense might become either the central element of a country's defense policy or a significant component within a broader, predominantly military, policy. There are at least four general models:

1. Full, relatively rapid, adoption of civilian-based defense as the country's defense policy by small countries that have no viable military or alliance alternative because of some special situation or condition.

2. The addition of a civilian-based component to a predominantly military defense policy to serve one or more specific purposes with no intent to expand that component to play wider roles within the overall policy.

3. The phased introduction and gradual expansion of civilian-based defense elements with the objective of eventual full transarmament.

4. The negotiated, phased, multilateral transarmament of several neighboring countries, simultaneously introducing civilian-based defense components, perhaps followed by a phased reduction of military weaponry.

Let us now look briefly in more detail at these possible models.

Full Rapid Adoption of Civilian-based Defense

Quick, full transarmament is most likely only for those countries that lack significant military options, or those for which the use of their military options would only bring certain devastation. Adoption of this policy might be possible for small countries that do not possess military forces, such as Costa Rica or Iceland. At present, such countries depend on either a very strong internal police force and the option of foreign assistance (Costa Rica) or membership in a foreign military alliance (Iceland). Both of these arrangements have disadvantages if real independence of action is a major objective.

Rapid adoption of the policy might also be possible for future newly independent countries (such as Palestine, Estonia, Latvia, Lithuania, Armenia, Hong Kong, or Tibet). These countries would possibly continue to feel threatened by their militarily more powerful neighbor (that is, previous ruler). However, there would be no way they could build up a self-reliant, adequate, military defense capacity. If the small country allied itself with a foreign military power, the former ruling government might well feel threatened or even provoked to invade. For countries in such situations, careful feasibility studies and thoughtful consideration may lead to civilian-based defense being seen as a realistic and more complete alternative to military policies. It would no longer be necessary to choose between making violent, but impotent, gestures or submitting passively to aggression or usurpation.

The ways in which civilian-based defense might be adopted by such newly independent countries might be more flexible than would be the case with longer-established state structures. In some cases, governmental initiatives in exploring civilian-based defense might precede consideration by the non-state institutions. Those initiatives might then provide the general framework for developing more specific plans. The population and institutions of the society could then evaluate the proposed defense policy and prepare for their roles in it.

In other cases, the initiative to adopt civilian-based defense might come from the population and the independent institutions of the society. This initiative, and even first preparations—potentially building on the experience of an independence struggle—could proceed prior to, or parallel with, governmental evaluation and decision making. In such cases, the recommendations of the independent institutions and occupational groups might then be integrated into a comprehensive national plan for a government-adopted policy.

Since civilian-based defense is a policy that projects defense potential on the basis of preparation and training beyond historical experience—as do innovations in most modern military weaponry—there are no examples of the adoption of civilian-based defense precisely on this model. However, the situation of Germany following the First World War is somewhat comparable. It still had military forces, but due to Treaty of Versailles provisions they were too weak to be a significant international factor. The German army, for several reasons, was even unwilling to act against the private armies of the *Freikorps* that attempted to overthrow the Weimar Republic in the Kapp Putsch of 1920. In 1923 the German military forces were too weak even to be sent into battle against the Belgian and French forces that had invaded the Ruhr. In both cases the government and political leaders initiated improvised nonviolent struggle for defense as the only realistic option.

Newly independent countries in the future should have considerable advantages over Germany's situation in the 1920s for several reasons: there is much more historical experience, the nature of nonviolent struggle and civilian-based defense is far better understood, and there is time for making preparations and training the population to wage the defense struggle.

Adding Civilian-based Components for Special Purposes

The general model usually presented by civilian-based defense theorists is for a full transarmament to the policy over a period of some years. These theorists have argued for full transarmament rather than a permanent combination of military and civilian-based defense on the basis of defense effectiveness. It is clear, however, that the interest in civilian-based defense is not limited to those few countries that initially contemplate a full changeover. There has been much more interest in the addition of civilian-based components to predominantly military policies.

When a civilian-based component is added to a predominantly military policy, there is no permanent commitment by the society or government to maintain that element at the initial level of operation and for the original specific purpose. That component might later be increased, reduced, or eliminated, depending on future assessments of its deterrence and defense capacity. Countries that have military options with reasonable chances of repelling invaders without incurring unacceptable casualties and destruction are likely to continue for a considerable time to rely on military means in case of attack. They may, however, at some point add a permanent civilian-based defense component to their predominantly military defense policy, as Sweden, Switzerland, Yugoslavia, and Austria have already done. In such cases there may also be other nonmilitary and paramilitary components.

For example, in April 1982 the Austrian Defense Minister Otto Rösch wrote: "The military portion of the national defense plan considers civilian resistance and therewith the forms of social defense as necessary complements to military national defense. In this context, these elements are systematically integrated in the ideological, civil, and economic areas of the *Umfassende Landesverteidigung* [General National Defense] and occupy a permanent position therein." The Austrian *Landesverteidigungsplan* (National Defense Plan), published in 1985, reaffirms that "civilian resistance is a necessary complement to the military national defense." It also states that in the event of a temporary occupation of portions of Austrian territory, "an organized civilian resistance," in full compliance with the international laws of war, could also be "effective" in supporting Austrian military fighting forces in the relevant area.

Sweden added a civilian-based component to its "total defense" policy in April 1986 by unanimous parliamentary vote. This followed approximately twenty years of discussions and investigations involving the parliament and the Ministry of Defense as well as political parties, academic researchers, religious bodies, and others. During 1981–1983 a commission—established by Cabinet decision—worked within the Ministry of Defense to prepare a plan for the use of "civil resistance" as part of the country's defense policy. The commission recommended that the "total defense" authorities should extend their planning to include "nonmilitary resistance" for territories that might be occupied in case of war. It also recommended establishment of a permanent commission that would initiate planning in stages, beginning with one of the six "High Regional Commands" that already coordinate other civilian components of the total defense policy. Basic and applied research and investigation of the relationships between military and nonmilitary defense were also recommended. A Commission on Nonmilitary Resistance was officially established on June 1, 1987, with these tasks: (1) to further the conditions for nonmilitary resistance through advice and recommendations to authorities and individuals; (2) to deal with questions of international law and psychological and other conditions of nonmilitary resistance, and (3) to further research in the field. The Commission's head, Gunnar Gustafsson, has written that preparations in peacetime for civil resistance "will achieve a valuable mental readiness" that should help make a potential aggressor "think carefully and perhaps abandon the original plans."

These cases, and others cited below, illustrate that nonviolent struggle for national defense is in certain countries accepted as an important component in overall national defense plans.

Civilian-based defense components would be intended to serve special purposes or to meet particular contingencies, while military means would be used for other situations. Such combinations of military-based and civilian-based defense are intended to be permanent; they are not viewed as transitionary steps toward full transarmament. These mixed policies would only be likely to change under one condition: if the society gained the confidence that civilian-based defense had a much greater potential for deterrence and defense than had been originally assessed.

Due to the very different dynamics and requirements for success of military action and nonviolent struggle, it is necessary to be clear about the role of a limited civilian-based defense component within a predominantly military defense policy. The identification of such specific purposes is crucial in the decision to adopt a civilian-based component. Three purposes of a special civilian-based component have been identified as:

1. the first line of defense in situations in which military resistance to invaders is obviously futile and suicidal

2. a reserve line of defense where military resistance has been used and has failed to repel invaders

3. as the main defense against internal usurpations, such as coups d'état.

Where military resistance is futile or suicidal. Some countries might base their assessment on whether to adopt partially civilian-based resistance on the relative military might of the potential attackers. If it is comparatively weak, the resistance might well be military. However, if the attackers' military capacity is overwhelming, military-based defense efforts would be obviously futile and suicidal. Then the civilian-based component could be employed as the first line of defense.

This was the situation in the two cases of improvised nonviolent resistance described in Chapter One, the German *Ruhrkampf* against French and Belgian invaders in 1923 and the Czechoslovak resistance against Warsaw Pact invaders in 1968. With increased knowledge, feasibility studies, and time for preparation and training, the effectiveness of such defense should be greatly increased. Therefore, a civilian-based component might be incorporated into the overall defense policy partly to deal with that specific contingency.

Where military resistance has failed. A civilian-based component might also be used where a country's military forces have attempted to repulse invaders but have been overwhelmed. This was the case in Norway during the German occupation, 1940–1945. The Dutch resistance against the Nazis is another important example.

In 1967, a study commissioned by the Norwegian Cabinet and prepared by the Norwegian Defense Research Institution contemplated the use of a prepared nonviolent resistance in case of the failure of military defense. "Nonviolent defense could accordingly be thought of as a type of defense in depth, should the protection [by military defense] of territorial integrity collapse." The report stated: "In case one assumes that a nonviolent defense in one form or another can be worked in as an addition to [the predominantly military] total defense, there is reasonable ground to assume that this will serve to strengthen Norway's resistance power and deterrence against enemy attack."

On March 1, 1989, the Norwegian Atlantic Committee sponsored a conference on "Complementary Forms of Defense." The introductory lecture on issues associated with an incorporation of civil resistance within Norway's "total defense" policy was presented by the Norwegian Defense Minister, Johan Jørgen Holst, who was a co-author of the 1967 report.

Such a component has been part of Swiss defense policy for some time. In the Swiss "general defense" policy, in case of a failure of the military forces to repel foreign attackers, both "armed resistance" (guerrilla and paramilitary struggle) and "passive resistance" would be used in occupied parts of the country.

Most of the population would not be participating in the violent resistance, however. Instead, citizens are instructed to refuse all collaboration while complying with international law. Although not resisting violently and not aiding such violence, this section of the population "nevertheless does not make the smallest concessions to the occupying power and disapproves every attempt at rapprochement." Refusal of collaboration, "the cold shoulder" against occupation personnel, and refusal of cooperation with all attempts to indoctrinate the population in the attackers' ideology are important responsibilities of the civilian population in this situation, as identified in the *Civilian Defense Book* issued in 1969 to every household in the country.

Finland is not among the countries that have already incorporated a nonviolent resistance component into its overall defense policy. However, in 1971 the presidentially supervised Finnish Psychological Defense Planning Commission issued the first official study of civilian-based defense. The commission rejected any complete replacement of military capacity by the new policy. However, the commission accepted the utility of adding a nonviolent resistance component to the country's predominantly military policy.

The report stated: "However, in certain crisis situations the methods of weaponless resistance can be practical as a supplement to armed resistance: they would come into question in an area which has come under the control of an invader. The examples gained from the experiences of various countries shows that these methods in combination with armed resistance can prove suitable during occupation in the effort to secure the freedom of action of social institutions and finally achieve liberation from occupation." After examining the possible beneficial uses of civilian-based defense, the 1971 Commission proposed that, alongside military preparations, Finland should make plans and prepare for nonviolent resistance in situations in which it is seen as a reasonable alternative, and that such work be initiated as quickly as possible. This was, however, not done.

Yugoslavia has already included a nonmilitary component in its Total National Defense policy. General Nikola Ljubicic writes that while military power is essential in a rational strategic system, "To win victory in an all-people's defense war, all types of resistance must be combined harmoniously and functionally, with armed struggle remaining the backbone." Yugoslav policy clearly allows for the use of nonviolent resistance in occupied parts of the country. "Naturally, units of the operational army and territorial defense may sometimes find themselves in the position of being forced temporarily to abandon further resistance and evacuate one or another town or settlement. But they must leave behind a military-political organization capable of continuing the struggle by political, diversionist and other forms of action."

As Adam Roberts has outlined, these other Yugoslav forms of resistance include: (1) moral, political, and psychological resistance—nonrecognition of capitulation and occupation, maintaining indigenous governmental structures, conducting agitation and propaganda, and the like; (2) economic resistance—production and supply for resistance forces, protection of property, refusal to perform work advantageous to the attacker, and so on; (3) resistance in culture and education; and (4) passive resistance—social boycotts, refusal to cooperate, and general attitude of noncompliance and hostility. The Yugoslav system of defense "calls for the total involvement of the political, economic, and social organizations. They are involved not only in executing plans, but also in formulating them."

Where a civilian-based component has been incorporated into a country's predominantly military defense posture, certain problems may arise. Persons and groups with major defense responsibilities will need to evaluate how the combination of military and nonviolent components is operating. For example, the resisters may wish to capitalize on the nonviolent character of a defense struggle in order to undermine the morale, reliability, and obedience of the attackers' troops (as occurred in Czechoslovakia in 1968). However, such efforts will be made exceptionally difficult or impossible if the same troops were previously under military attack, if some of their friends were killed or wounded, or if they currently fear for their own lives.

The problems of combining violent and nonviolent techniques are especially acute in proposals that would use both guerrilla warfare and nonviolent struggle within the same overall defense strategy. Several recent "defensive defense" or "nonoffensive defense" models, as mentioned in Chapter One, contain this problem. If nonviolent resistance and guerrilla warfare are used simultaneously by resisters in the same geographical area, exceptionally serious problems could arise, not only leading to very high casualties but also completely undermining the effectiveness of nonviolent struggle as well. For these reasons, the addition of a civilian-based defense component to a military defense policy should not be accompanied by the addition of guerrilla warfare or certain "defensive defense" military components.

A mixed defense policy with both military and civilian components is a clear advance from an exclusively military-based policy. However, continuing attention to the inconsistencies that can arise and their consequences will be required as the overall policy develops. If studies of the civilian-based defense policy and experience in its development and practice demonstrate greater defense capacity than had originally existed or been perceived, these problems can potentially be resolved by progressive movement toward full transarmament. Otherwise, great care must be taken to prevent the undermining by the military component of the very factors that contribute to success by the civilian-based component. In general, the problems will be less acute if it is possible to separate or isolate the operations of the military-based and civilian-based defense systems.

Against internal usurpations. Another possible model of partial transarmament is the addition of a civilian-based defense component specifically to prevent and defeat coups d'état, executive usurpations, or other unconstitutional attempts to seize control of the state apparatus. Internal attacks constitute a serious defense problem. Dozens of societies during recent decades have seen their constitutional democratic governments—and other systems—thrown out of power, their political leaders killed, and a new dictatorial government imposed by the threat or use of military force.

In some countries, such as Thailand, efforts to achieve greater democracy and social justice have been repeatedly disrupted by military or political coups over several decades. In some Latin American countries, such as Argentina, Peru, Chile, Guatemala, and Brazil, coups have produced grave problems in past decades. In African countries, where the military organizations are clearly better organized and more powerful than much of the civil society, coups d'état have been a major factor in shaping the political systems of the continent since their independence. Europe has had its share of coups in past decades as well.

Quite diverse countries might therefore want quickly to adopt civilian-based defense, if only for preventing internal usurpations, while retaining military options for dealing with international dangers.

Most coups d'état are often largely or purely military operations. Other coups are attempted seizures of the state by dictatorial political parties or "intelligence" bodies; sometimes coups are conducted or supported by combinations of civilian and military groups.

Declaring such seizures to be illegal or unconstitutional is no solution to this problem: their perpetrators are quite willing to violate standing constitutional and legal prohibitions. Few people are willing to resort to civil war to block such attempts. Besides, when the military forces themselves are conducting or backing the coup, the chances of a military victory by civilians wanting to defend the constitution are extremely small. Except in those cases in which the putschists are only a small group without much support and the military forces are overwhelmingly loyal to the constitutional government, there is no military answer to this problem, just as there is no constitutional solution.

Civilian-based defense is potentially the only policy to block establishment of a dictatorship that does not risk civil war. The two cases described in Chapter One—Germany in 1920 and France in 1961—were successful. This suggests that the basic answer to the problem of blocking internal usurpations may lie in a refined and developed policy that builds on the essential characteristics of those cases.

The basic pattern of civilian-based defense against such usurpations would approximate the operations described in Chapter Four: denying legitimacy to the attackers; seeking to prevent them from establishing a government and effective administration; keeping control of the civil service, police, and military forces out of the attackers' hands; mobilizing the institutions and public of the civil society to refuse to accept governance by the usurpers; attempting to subvert the troops and supporters of the usurpers; and attempting to gain maximum international nonviolent backing for the restoration of constitutional government.

Preparations—of the society, the governmental apparatus, and the citizenry—can be made to develop the capacity to defeat such attacks by noncooperation and defiance. Those countries that have experienced such usurpations in the past should be especially attentive to this possibility. That does not mean that other countries without such a record should be indifferent. In the United States the 1987 "Irangate" investigations revealed the existence of a small group—including the then director of the Central Intelligence Agency—intent on establishing a self-sustaining, powerful, "secret government" to do what it thought desirable and necessary regardless of the constitutional procedures and institutions of the U.S. government. This should be a serious warning that very few, if any, governments are immune to attempted internal take-overs and subversion.

In most cases, regimes and societies that feel themselves to be vulnerable to such usurpations can launch the same types of investigation, public discussion, policy consideration, and decision making as would be used for adoption of civilian-based defense for other purposes. Specific legislation and public education should establish a moral and legal responsibility of everyone to refuse to support and obey any group seeking to abolish the constitutional system and impose themselves as the new rulers.

Under certain political conditions, however, if governmental consideration and preparations for defense against internal usurpations are not made through the usual channels, another model exists. The policy against usurpations can be discussed by the public through a widespread program of public education using, for example, newspapers, magazines, handbooks, radio, and television, and by the institutions of the society (loci of power). These organizations would not be limited to educational, social, religious, trade union, business, cultural, and similar elements of the society. They should also include government officials, civil servants, police, soldiers, political party members, and other groups. This could produce a situation in which the nature of civilian-based defense would be widely known throughout the society, and basic responsibilities and specific defense responses would be well understood. Under these conditions it should be possible to prevent an unconstitutional seizure of power.

The adoption of civilian-based defense only for the purpose of maintaining constitutional government against internal usurpation can play an extremely important role. This aspect of the policy should be of interest to most governments of the world. Regardless of the ways many of them came to power, they often learn that to retain power they require legitimacy and popular acceptance, and have no wish to be themselves summarily thrown out by a coup d'état.

Planning for Phased Full Transarmament

There are a number of countries whose military capacity, when compared to potential attackers, is so limited that they are incapable of serious military defense. The military may serve a largely symbolic role in some countries, or have only the capacity for repressive action in times of acute domestic crisis in others. Limited military capacity can occur for various reasons, including limited domestic resources, economic limitations, small population, and the like. In some countries, such as Austria, domestic considerations may be made more complex by international treaty limitations.

Poland, on the other hand, might be capable of supporting a larger military system, given a solution of the economic problems, but it could never be adequate against the Soviet Union or NATO forces. (Indeed, the main use of the Polish military forces in the 1980s was for internal repression.) A similar situation could exist for the increasingly independent and democratic countries of Eastern Europe, such as Czechoslovakia, East Germany, and Bulgaria.

Such countries as these might well give very serious consideration to long-range full transarmament. An essential acceptance of the goal of full transarmament might be made, or at least widely accepted, early in the process, but the transition would most likely be deliberately phased to operate over some time, such as a ten or fifteen year period.

Actual transarmament for these countries would most likely begin with incorporation of limited civilian-based components into exclusively or predominantly military policies. This would involve implementation of preparation and training and mobilization of defense capacity throughout the society's institutions. By beginning with limited civilian-based components, the society and government would gain experience in how to prepare, train, and conduct this type of defense. The initial components might then be gradually expanded and new ones added, assuming that preparations and experience indicated sufficient viability for the policy. As this capacity and confidence increases, it would be possible gradually to reduce reliance on military components until full transarmament was accomplished.

Full transarmament for such countries would have several advantages. First, they would not be military threats to their neighbors. Second, they would have enhanced deterrence and defense capacities. And third, they would virtually have eliminated the possibility of an internal coup d'état or executive usurpation by military means, while having mobilized the capacity to defeat any such attacks. The defense needs and domestic situations of certain countries are sufficiently serious, and the development of nonviolent struggle for defense and liberation sufficiently promising, that we should not be surprised when significant political steps are taken in this direction.

Multilateral Transarmament

Civilian-based defense has always been proposed as a policy that could be adopted by unilateral decision in approximately the same way that governments have added new military weapons, or have shifted to whole new weapons systems. Because the new weaponry was seen as *increasing* the combat power of the military forces, there was no need, or advantage, to negotiating agreements with neighboring regimes or hostile governments—requiring them also to adopt the new weapons. This has been the case with every change in military weaponry that has ever been adopted. On the other hand, there have been many attempts to *reduce* the quantity or type of military weaponry by treaties and negotiated agreements. In the long run, these have not been notably successful.

If civilian-based defense is really a powerful policy for deterring and defending against attacks, then there is no reason for any country to wait to transarm—in part or in full—until its neighbors and potential attackers are also willing to do so. It is possible, however, that some type of multilateral, phased, partial or full transarmament might be a viable option in certain situations. This option might be implemented without formal negotiations and treaties, while in other cases those measures would be an important part of the change in defense and military capacities.

The multilateral introduction of civilian-based components, and their progressive expansion, might well occur in certain regions, such as the Nordic countries, Central America, or Central Europe. The basis is already laid for some serious research and policy studies on the potential of civilian-based components in the defense policies of four of the five Nordic countries—Sweden, Norway, Denmark, and Finland. Little, or nothing, has been done in Iceland, however.

Central America is a region where there has been little serious governmental interest in civilian-based defense. It is also a region where military forces have bolstered or created military and political dictatorships, and where neighboring governments have at times threatened or conducted aggression. One way in which the likelihood of international tensions and internal dictatorships might be reduced is through the phased introduction of civilian-based defense components, perhaps followed by reductions of various types of military weaponry and forces. The strengthening of civil institutions would be a vital element in introducing the new defense policy in this region.

Transarmament by international negotiation might be arranged in Central Europe, especially in light of the major changes which have taken place in Eastern Europe and the widespread reassessments of defense and security policies among Western European countries. Civilian-based defense might provide the missing link that would facilitate major military reductions at least, if not full demilitarization, of a broad corridor from Northern to Southern Europe. The civilian-based components could be phased in on agreed schedules followed by reductions in the type and quantity of military armaments. When defense capacity can be retained while an agreed process of demilitarization proceeds, some of the barriers to negotiated arms reduction and disarmament are removed.

Civilian-based Defense and the Superstates

Much less attention has been given to the applicability of civilian-based defense to present and potential superstates than to the defense problems of small and medium-size countries. Superstates today most obviously include the United States and the Soviet Union. This status is not primarily based on their possession of nuclear weapons, rather it is derived from the vastness of their territories and populations, and the size of their state structures. In that context, China and India also belong in this category. A united Europe would also be a superstate, though significantly differing from all the others. In addition to land size and population, the degree of centralized control and the extent of military capacity are additional important criteria.

The applicability of civilian-based defense in the case of superstates depends to a considerable degree on the assessment of the nature of these regimes and their objectives. Many people would, with evidence and rationale, view one or more of these large states as being primarily aggressive or oppressive, seeking to dominate its neighbors, to maintain rigid central control over its own population, or to direct the politics, economics, and military policies of distant countries. If that is the case, such a superstate would be seen as a likely aggressor against which civilian-based defense and other expressions of nonviolent struggle must be waged.

On the other hand, to the degree that a superstate's aggressive foreign activity and internal repression is seen to be a defensive reaction to perceived international threats, then civilian-based defense might become a positive contribution to the development of those societies and to a reduction of the more offensive characteristics of that superstate. According to Josef Stalin, the necessity to deal with foreign threats made the ideal of a workers' democracy "impossible." Stalin used arguments of national security against pleas for freedom of discussion within the Communist Party. He also argued that "to free the state from bureaucratic elements . . . a completely secure, peaceful condition all around" is needed "so that we would not need large military cadres . . . which put their imprint on the other governmental institutions."

There are several ways that civilian-based defense may be useful to superstates. It is assumed that, because of their total reliance on vast military resources, these states are incapable for the present time of conducting full transarmament, either on the quick-changeover or the long-term model. Initially, therefore, the points of practical relevance of this policy for superstates are likely to be as supplementary components within predominantly military policies, as a means of blocking coups d'état or as policies for their previously dependent allies.

Let us focus discussion briefly on the potential of civilian-based defense for superstates on the United States and the Soviet Union. Their situations have both similarities and significant differences.

If present dependent allies of the United States—especially Western European countries and Japan—are able to assume full, or at least primary, responsibility for their own defense through this new policy, that would greatly reduce U.S. military expenditures—perhaps by half! To that end, the United States could encourage its allies to investigate civilian-based defense and perhaps assist them by sharing research results, feasibility studies, and other knowledge about the policy. European and Japanese transarmament would also vastly simplify the security problems for the United States.

With the need to defend those dependent allies removed, the major security threats for the United States would then theoretically be reduced to three: nuclear war, invasion, and internal usurpation. The technical and logistical problems of a military invasion and occupation of the continental United States are so vast that it is virtually a nonproblem. Even minimal civilian-based defense preparations would sufficiently increase the problems of a foreign occupation to eliminate that threat. Civilian-based defense preparations would be needed to deter and defend against internal takeovers by coup d'état, executive usurpation, or "secret government," as already noted. That would leave only the very serious, continuing problem of potential attack by nuclear and other weapons of mass destruction. Significant steps have already been taken in the direction of reducing that threat by combinations of multilateral agreements and unilateral actions. Reduction of motives for such attacks would also be important. In short, civilian-based defense would not remove or solve all of the security problems of the United States, but it has the potential of vastly simplifying them and effectively dealing with some of the most serious ones.

What, then, of the Soviet Union? If the peoples and political leaders of the Soviet Union genuinely wish to democratize and decentralize, then civilian-based defense could become highly relevant to meeting its own security needs. Assuming that the democratizing trends continue in the Soviet Union and Eastern Europe, civilian-based defense constitutes a way for Eastern European countries to become more independent of Soviet controls without becoming a military threat to the Soviet Union. Transarmament of Eastern European countries would also pave the way for the Soviet Union to reduce the great weight of its military expenditures as its neighbors assume greater responsibility for their own defense.

The same also applies to the nationalities problem within the Soviet Union. For example, suppose that some nations now incorporated in the Soviet Union, such as Estonia, Latvia, Lithuania, Armenia, and Georgia, become independent. To reduce military threats to the Soviet Union, the newly independent countries could, as a condition of independence, be required to remain demilitarized and be prohibited from joining military alliances. Civilian-based defense would be a potentially sensible policy for them.

In regard to potential aggression against the Soviet Union, the problems of a successful military invasion and occupation are already so vast that a well-prepared civilian-based defense policy could constitute a powerful deterrent and an effective defense against such attacks. This policy would be compatible with progress in internal democratization, decentralization, and shifting economic and manpower resources to make significant, much-needed improvements in the material conditions of the population.

The Soviet Union, as most states, is vulnerable to internal usurpations, especially because of the high degree of centralization of the present system. This type of attack might be launched by neo-Stalinists opposed to *glasnost* and *perestroika* and intent on restoring strong central controls, or by military or political groups wishing to reimpose an authoritarian system of some other type. In case of a coup, a civilian-based defense capacity could be the only effective deterrence and defense that a democratized Soviet Union would have.

The situations of other superstates and large countries, such as China, India, a united Europe, and the like, are very different. Examinations of the relevance of civilian-based defense to their security needs are urgently needed.

Potential Benefits of a Civilian-based Defense Policy

In the long-run, civilian-based defense has the potential of producing various benefits that are not possible with military defense policies. These advantages are discussed below.

1. Civilian-based defense would increase the capacity for self-reliance in defense and security matters, even by small and medium-size

countries, by shifting the decisive factor from military to societal strength. Dependency on foreign countries for military weapons and supplies and alliances with militarily more powerful states would then no longer be required. The financial and political costs of such dependency are thereby removed.

More importantly, self-defense, if possible, is always more reliable than dependence on allies, who in a crisis may not come to one's aid as promised. Witness Czechoslovakia abandoned by her allies in 1939, and invaded by her allies in 1968! Civilian-based defense provides the fullest possible self-reliance in deterrence and defense, while reducing the risks of war.

2. By its nonmilitary nature civilian-based defense provides deterrence and defense capacities without the foreign attack capabilities of military systems, thereby reducing international anxieties and dangers.

Internationally, many of the military weapons that may have been procured, or justified, for purposes of deterring and defending against attacks can also be used to attack other countries. That reality has often, with or without justification, increased international tensions, exacerbated arms races, and heightened the prospects of war. In contrast, civilian-based defense is able to provide deterrence and defense without the capacity to launch military attacks on other countries.

3. As civilian-based defense becomes more widely adopted, successful, and recognized as powerful, the incidence of international military aggression is likely to be reduced. Potential attackers are likely to be deterred from aggression against other countries.

The prospect of having to deal with countries that have made themselves politically indigestible, capable of denying the attackers their objectives, and able to sow disaffection among the attacking forces, is likely to cause aggressors to have second thoughts and to lead to abandonment of at least some cases of aggression. This effect is likely to increase with the expansion of the numbers of countries adopting civilian-based defense, and the accumulation of evidence from actual civilian-based defense struggles that well-prepared countries will be difficult or impossible to defeat.

4. Civilian-based defense may reduce nuclear proliferation by providing an alternative route to self-reliance in security policies where conventional military means are perceived to be inadequate or impracticable.

One reason—not the only one—why some states are interested in developing a nuclear weapons capacity is that they see their conventional military means to be insufficient and want to avoid dependency on the weaponry and policies of military superpowers. Civilian-based defense provides an alternative route, a way around nuclear weapons to achieve independence in deterrence and defense. If this is understood, increasing adoption of this policy may reduce nuclear proliferation.

5. Civilian-based defense is likely to reduce the incidence of internal usurpations and internal suppression by military forces. One of the great ironies for supporters of democratic governments has been that in many countries, and under widely differing conditions, the military forces that have been created to *defend* that society and government have themselves turned to *attack* it. In dozens of countries the military forces have thrown out the constitutional government and installed a military government. Or, military "defense" forces have been used to bolster dictatorships and to suppress domestic movements for greater freedom and social justice, and even to perpetrate massacres (such as by the British in Amritsar in 1919 and the Chinese in Tiananmen Square in 1989).

This is not the case with civilian-based defense. In the first place, in contrast to military systems, civilian-based defense does not build up an internal violent capacity for carrying out a coup d'état against a legitimated constitutional government. In the second place, the preparations for noncooperation and defiance required by a civilian-based defense policy actually create a deterrence and constitutional defense capacity against internal usurpations. Furthermore, due to their nonviolent nature, the weapons of civilian-based defense cannot generally be used for purposes of repression. If nonviolent struggle is used in internal conflicts, it can be disruptive, but the results are generally compatible with internal peace and order, and the consequences of internal violence are avoided.

As the discussions in Chapters One and Four have shown, civilian-based defense is designed to defend against these internal attacks as well as foreign aggression. This is something that military means usually cannot do without risking civil war, unless the would-be putschists are a discredited small minority. Unfortunately, in far more cases the military forces, police, and bureaucracy often assist or at least go along with the coup, whether for reasons of genuine support, a desire to avoid civil war, or lack of knowledge of what else they can do. Civilian-based defense provides a powerful means of combatting internal usurpations without initiating widespread internal violence.

6. Adopting and preparing for a civilian-based defense policy may, under some conditions at least, contribute to a reduction of internal violence by groups with grievances and indirectly encourage them to express their claims by nonviolent forms of action.

Internal violence may derive from deep differences of ideology and from the frustrations of suffering injustices, oppression, and poverty.

Such violence may take the form of rioting, assassinations, terrorism, or guerrilla warfare. The practitioners of violence may justify themselves by citing the severity of the issues at stake and by the conviction that violence is the most powerful means of action available. This latter argument is given credence by the society's commitment to military action to deal with extreme international and domestic crises. Thus, that evaluation and legitimization of violence for "good" causes, such as national defense, may have unanticipated and unrecognized influences on how some acute domestic conflicts are conducted. People with strong grievances may feel justified in employing violence because other means seem to have failed and because their society has given its imprimatur to using organized violence to settle severe conflicts.

As a result of transarmament, violence is no longer endorsed by the society as the most powerful type of action that can be taken. Instead, nonviolent struggle is seen as a more effective course of action. The legitimacy that had been given to violence for good causes is taken away and given instead to nonviolent struggle.

7. Civilian-based defense is more likely than its military counterpart to keep attention focused on the original objectives of the conflict rather than on the damage inflicted on the enemy.

One of the tragedies of military warfare has been that it operates primarily on the basis of how much destruction and how many deaths can be inflicted on the enemy forces, population, and homeland. The original issues in the conflict usually take a back seat to the means of action seen to be required to wage the war. Frequently, military victory is gained while the deeper goals of the conflict are forgotten.

A very different dynamic operates in nonviolent struggle. Acts of nonviolent protest and resistance are usually most effective if they are themselves expressions of the issues at stake. Resistance to censorship may often be best implemented, for example, by the defiant exercise of free speech and a free press rather than by killing members of the government that ordered the censorship.

8. Civilian-based defense, in common with nonviolent struggle more generally, tends to produce fewer casualties and less destruction than comparable military conflicts. That has major advantages.

While we do not have detailed statistical studies, all the available evidence indicates that the numbers of dead and wounded, not to mention the amount of physical damage, during conventional wars, and especially guerrilla wars, are vastly higher than in comparable nonviolent struggles. That takes into consideration the gravity of the issues at stake, the size of populations, and other factors.

9. By dispensing with conventional and nuclear attack capacities, countries with a civilian-based defense are far less likely to be threatened or attacked with weapons of mass destruction.

Ironically, present means of nuclear deterrence—intended to deter attacks—have the effect of inducing other nuclear powers to target countries with such weapons or, in extreme crises, even to launch preemptive strikes against them, precisely because such countries are potential attackers.

10. The likelihood of foreign attack may also be reduced by the development of a more "positive" foreign policy, which can strengthen a civilian-based defense by reducing international hostilities and increasing goodwill toward the country with the nonmilitary policy.

A civilian-based defense policy is more likely than a military policy to facilitate these changes. The shift would also make more economic resources available for the domestic civilian economy and for providing international assistance. Financial, material, and personnel resources would no longer be tied to meeting military requirements and could therefore be more available for helping to meet human needs in one's own and other countries. More resources could also be freed to help resolve international problems short of violent conflict.

While such assistance should be undertaken for its own sake, it is advantageous for countries with civilian-based defense policies to win increased international goodwill by such means, goodwill that may both discourage attack and bring international support in case of aggression. Such mutually supportive policies accompanying transarmament are likely to contribute to increasing one's own national security and to improving human conditions internationally.

11. A civilian-based defense policy would also reduce the size of government and the expense of deterrence and defense. Since wars and military systems have been major factors in the vast growth of the state, this shift to a nonmilitary system of defense would help to reverse the general tendency to expand the size, and costs, of government and the defense establishment.

While a civilian-based policy would have significant economic costs, it would be far less expensive than a military-based policy. This is primarily because civilian-based defense does not require military hardware. Additionally, defense responsibilities are shifted from large, professional military systems to the general population and the society's independent institutions. This would not exclude the existence of professional civilian-based defense research centers, strategic planning groups, bodies working on aspects of preparation and training, for example, but they would be much smaller than military forces usually are. There would also be a strong tendency for a major part of the civilian-based defense to be conducted through the independent organizations and institutions of the society, rather than through vast special cadres.

12. Civilian-based defense would remove the centralizing influences endemic to military systems and, instead, introduce decentralizing influences associated with nonviolent sanctions. These would especially include the development of increased self-reliance. These influences toward self-reliance would contribute to the development of a less centralist and more pluralist social and political structure, with greater popular participation, promoting the diffusion of power and responsibility throughout the society. All this is, of course, compatible with the ideals of democratic systems.

13. Another benefit of a civilian-based defense policy would be to stimulate the citizenry to evaluate the principles espoused by their society and to assess how it stands up to those standards. By placing responsibility for defense on the people themselves, this policy would encourage citizens to recognize qualities of the society worthy of defense and to consider how their society could be improved.

14. By providing deterrence and defense by civilian forms of struggle, the new policy provides a way by which war can be incrementally replaced with a less dangerous option. When that option is seen to be adequate, whole countries can then abandon military means because they would no longer be needed. A gradual reduction in reliance on military means becomes realistic to the degree that the new civilian-based defense policy is demonstrated to be capable of providing genuine deterrence and defense capacity. Single countries, or groups of countries, can take significant steps toward the abandonment of war by the development and progressive substitution of its political equivalent.

Further Consideration of This Option

The potential of a civilian-based defense policy needs to be examined and discussed widely among the population and institutions of all societies with an internal or external defense problem. That means, in effect, virtually all countries. While in some cases the initiative may come from the government or even the military forces, it is much more likely that the discussions will begin among the people, within various independent institutions, and among scholarly researchers and policy analysts.

Various steps can be taken to spread knowledge of the nature and potential of this option throughout the society and to promote more widespread official and nongovernmental evaluation of the policy. The aim of these activities should be to extend knowledge, stimulate thought, and encourage a continuing evaluation of the practical potential of this policy. The effort should *not* be to gain converts or "believers."

A basic first step is self-education by individuals and small study groups to gain or expand knowledge of civilian-based defense and to help them to assess their judgments about the need for further exploration and development of this policy. Individuals may wish to increase their own skills—as in public speaking and writing—to improve their effectiveness in educational efforts, or to continue their higher education to prepare themselves for research and policy analysis in this field.

Nonviolent struggle and civilian-based defense ought to be included in the subject matter of broader courses within our educational systems, and special courses on these subjects need to be introduced or expanded. Their aim should be to disseminate knowledge and stimulate students to think for themselves—not to come to a particular opinion.

Financial resources are urgently needed to assist the research, policy studies, educational work, and public outreach about the nature and potential of nonviolent struggle generally and civilian-based defense in particular. Local, state, regional, national, and international organizations might establish special commissions to study civilian-based defense with a view to recommending whether this policy merits further attention or action by the parent body.

At key points when the needed public groundwork has advanced sufficiently, committees of legislatures, parliaments, national assemblies and the like can conduct private and public investigations of this option, and similar investigations can and should be undertaken by defense departments and ministries and other military organizations.

The present dangers of international aggression and internal usurpations, on the one hand, and of military responses to them, on the other, are severe. As suggested in this book, significant evidence exists that the potential of civilian-based defense may be substantial. The contention here is that civilian-based defense could successfully deter and defend against those attacks without precipitating the dangers and costs of international and civil war.

This alternative policy is, however, in its nascent stage, and greater knowledge and understanding of its problems and potential are required. It should, therefore, be thoroughly investigated. Feasibility studies for particular countries and threats ought to be undertaken, since the needs, potentialities, and problems of defense vary widely from country to country.

Consideration and phased adoption of civilian-based defense components are likely to continue to grow, in part due to the increasingly obvious limitations on the real usefulness of military options for defense in many countries. Attention to civilian-based defense is also likely to expand because of the greatly increasing use of nonviolent struggle throughout the world.

It is time that these efforts be accelerated and vastly expanded. At worst, they would reveal this to be a dead-end idea, on which no further attention and resources should be wasted. A moderate result of those efforts would be the demonstration that, while unable at this time to deal effectively with certain contingencies, civilian-based defense could at least make important contributions to deterrence and defense in place of military options. At best, the investigations would reveal that civilian-based defense has a much greater potential than has been recognized and that, minimally, it may play a major role in future defense policies. The power of the people may finally prove to be the strongest and safest system of defense—a post-military defense.

Notes

For a related discussion of transarmament, see Gene Sharp, *Making Europe Unconquerable* (London: Taylor & Francis, 1985, and Cambridge, Mass.: Ballinger Publishers, 1985; second American edition, with a forward by George Kennan, Cambridge, Mass.: Ballinger Publishers, 1986), chapter three.

The quotation from the Austrian Defense Minister, Otto Rösch, is contained in a letter he sent Dr. Andreas Maislinger, April 30, 1982. I thank Dr. Maislinger for this information.

For information on the role of civilian resistance in Austrian defense policy, see *Landesverteidigungsplan* (National Defense Plan) (Vienna: Federal Chancellery, March 1985), pp. 49 and 55. I thank Dr. Heinz Vetschera for supplying extensive documents on Austria's defense policy and consideration of a civilian-based defense component.

The tasks of the Swedish Commission on Nonmilitary Resistance are outlined in the Swedish Government ordinance, "SFS 1987:199 Förordning med instruktion för delegationen för icke-militärt motstånd," April 23, 1987. I would like to thank Lennart Bergfeldt for this and other information on nonmilitary resistance in Sweden. In addition, I thank the Swedish Ministry of Defense and its military attaché in Washington, D.C., for extensive documentation.

The quote from Gunnar Gustafsson is taken from his introduction to Håkan Wall's *Motstånd utan våld* (Resistance Without Violence) (Stockholm: Sveriges Utbildningsradio AB [Swedish Educational Broadcasting Company], 1988), pp. 2 and 3.

For further information on the Norwegian resistance to the Nazi occupation, see Gene Sharp, *Tyranny Could Not Quell Them* (London: Peace News, 1958, and later editions), pamphlet. On the Dutch resistance to the Germans, see Werner Warmbrunn, *The Dutch Under German Occupation 1940–1945*, (Palo Alto, Ca.: Stanford University Press and London: Oxford University Press, 1963).

For the 1967 Norwegian study, see Johan Jørgen Holst, Eystein Fjærli, and Harald Rønning, "Ikke-Militært Forsvar og Norsk Sikkerhetspolitikk" (Nonmilitary Defense and Norwegian Security Policy) (Kjeller, Norway: Forsvarets Forskningsinstitutt [Defense Research Institute], 1967), pp. 44 and 46.

The quotations on Swiss civilian actions in case of an occupation are from Albert Bachmann and Georges Grosjean, *Zivilverteidigung* (Civilian Defense) (Miles-Verlag, Aarau: Eidg. Justiz- und Polizeidepartement im Auftrag des Bundesrates [Confederal Justice and Police Departments by order of the Federal Council], 1969) pp. 273–300.

The information on Finland is taken from "Aseeton Vastarinta" (Weaponless Resistance) (Helsinki: Henkisen maanpuolustuksen suunnittelukunta, 1971), mimeograph pp. 27–28. In 1975, a second Finnish report was issued, accepting the usefulness of "weaponless resistance" as a supplement to the armed resistance. See "Aseeton Vastarinta ja sen toteuttamisedellytykset Suomessa" (Helsinki: Henkisen maanpuolustuksen suunnittelukunta, 1975), mimeograph p. 29. I am grateful to Steven Huxley for research and translation of cited Finnish documents.

The quotation from General Nikola Ljubicic is taken from his book, *Total National Defense—Strategy of Peace* (Belgrade: Socialist Thought and Practice, 1977), p. 151.

The quote on the continuation of resistance after the cessation of military defense in the event of an occupation of parts of Yugoslavia, is from Lt.-Col. Milojica Pantelic, "Territorial Defense," in Vukotic et al., *The Yugoslav Concept of General People's Defense* (Belgrade: Medunarodna Politika), p. 280, and is cited in Adam Roberts, *Nations in Arms*, second edition (New York: St. Martin's Press, 1986), p. 210.

The outline of nonmilitary forms of resistance in Yugoslavia is taken from an article, "Forms of Resistance in Nationwide Defense," *Svenarodna Odbrana* (Zagreb) (August–September 1972), as cited in Roberts, *Nations in Arms*, pp. 210–211.

See Roberts, *Nations in Arms*, p. 179, for the quote on the role of political, social, and economic organizations in planning and implementing Yugoslav defense.

On the "Irangate" investigations and the revelation of a "secret government," see *Report of the Congressional Committees Investigating the Iran-Contra Affair*, abridged edition (New York: Random House, 1988).

On Stalin's views on the impact of military threats on internal dictatorship, see Isaac Deutscher, *Stalin: A Political Biography* (London: Oxford University Press, 1959), pp. 226, 258, 263, and 285.

On the potential of civilian-based defense to make European members of NATO more self-reliant and to reduce the military role of the United States, see Sharp, *Making Europe Unconquerable*.

For Further Reading on Civilian-based Defense

Brigadier General Edward B. Atkeson, "The Relevance of Civilian-based Defense to U.S. Security Interests," *Military Review*, Fort Leavenworth, Kansas, vol. 56, no. 5 (May 1976), pp. 24–32, and no. 6 (June 1976), pp. 45–55.

Adam Roberts, "Civil Resistance to Military Coups," *Journal of Peace Research* (Oslo), vol. XII, no. 1 (1975), pp. 19–36.

————, editor, *Civilian Resistance as a National Defense: Nonviolent Action Against Aggression* (Harrisburg, Pa.: Stackpole Books, 1968); reprint of *The Strategy of Civilian Defence* (London: Faber & Faber, 1967). Paperback edition with a new introduction, *Civilian Resistance as a National Defense: Nonviolent Action Against Aggression* (Harmondsworth, England, and Baltimore, Md.: Penguin Books, 1969). All out of print.

Gene Sharp, "Making the Abolition of War a Realistic Goal," pamphlet, Ira D. and Miriam G. Wallach Award essay (New York: World Policy Institute, 1980).

————, *Making Europe Unconquerable* (London: Taylor and Francis, 1985, and Cambridge, Mass.: Ballinger, 1985; second American edition, with a forward by George Kennan, Cambridge, Mass.: Ballinger, 1986).

————, *National Security Through Civilian-Based Defense*, booklet (Omaha: Civilian-based Defense Association, formerly Association for Transarmament Studies, 1985).

————, " 'The Political Equivalent of War'—Civilian-based Defense," in Gene Sharp, *Social Power and Political Freedom* (Introduction by Senator Mark O. Hatfield), Boston, Mass.: Porter Sargent, 1980).

For a selected multilingual bibliography of literature on civilian-based defense to 1985, see Sharp, *Making Europe Unconquerable*, pp. 165–171, in the second American edition.

Also of Interest

Gene Sharp, *Gandhi as a Political Strategist, with Essays on Ethics and Politics*, Introduction by Coretta Scott King (Cambridge, Mass.: Porter Sargent 1979).

————, *The Politics of Nonviolent Action*, Introduction by Thomas C. Schelling, three volumes (Cambridge, Mass.: Porter Sargent, 1973). The three volumes in paperback from the same publisher are: *Power and Struggle*, *The Methods of Nonviolent Action*, and *The Dynamics of Nonviolent Action*.

For information on other books (including various foreign translations) on nonviolent struggle and civilian-based defense, and for information on the Albert Einstein Institution, of which Gene Sharp is president write: Publications, The Albert Einstein Institution, 1430 Massachusetts Avenue, Cambridge, Massachusetts 02138.

Index

7; controlling of, 29; defined, 22; degree of availability of, 25; dependent on co-operation and obedience, 23, 25; depends on cooperation of individuals and institutions, 26; human resources and, 24; and implementation of power-theory, 30–31; intangible factors and, 24; material resources and, 25; nonviolent action/struggle and, 48; potential of, 22; sanctions and, 25; skills and knowledge and, 24; sources of, 23–25; theory of, 22; withdrawal of sources of, 23, 24, 26. *See also* sources of power

Popular empowerment, 123

Quisling, Vidkun, 67

Reitlinger, Gerald, 55

Repression, 23, 27, 109; aims to produce submission, 96; application of, requires cooperation, 27, 28–29; against civilian defenders, 95, 108; as counterproductive to repressor, 57; as evidence of threat to opponent, 55; as exposing violent nature of opponents' system, 55; fear of, produces obedience, 28; immobilizing agencies of, 57; insufficient to insure cooperation, 27–29; insufficient to maintain regime, 27; limitations on, against nonviolent action/struggle, 54; as no reason to panic, 57; as response to noncooperation, 27; of strikes, 70. *See also* political jiujitsu; sanctions

Roberts, Adam, 135

Rösch, Otto, 131

Royal Garhwal Rifles, British India, 67

Ruhrkampf, 9, 14–16, 42, 43, 107, 109, 121, 131, 133; *advocats des boches* in, 15–16; assassinations of suspected informers in, 15; Belgian and French popular support during, 15; demolitions in, 15; described, 14–16; exploitation of coal in, 92; Franco-Belgian objectives in, 86; government policy of nonviolent resistance in, 14; informers in, 15; methods of resistance in, 15; political noncooperation in, 45; protest strike in, 43; repression in, 15, 59; results of, 73; sabotage in, 15, 94; spies in, 15; trade unions support of noncooperation during, 14

Rulers: defined, 22; dependent on sources of power, 25; limits on power of, 32; power not intrinsic to, 22, 23; sources of power of, 23; variations in power of, 32. *See also* political power; sources of power

Rumania, 54

Russia: 1905 Great October Strike, 63; 1905 massacre of protesters in St. Petersburg, 59; 1905 Revolution, 8, 49; 1917 Bolshevik coup d'état, 48; 1917 February Revolution, 8, 64, 71; 1917 Revolution, 48; Bureau of Zemstvo Congresses, 47; Duma of Imperial, 63; Ochrana, 57; Provisional Government in, 48; repression in 1917 February Revolution, 59

Sabotage: in *Ruhrkampf*, 15; repression and, 94

Salan, General, 12

Sanctions, 23, 24, 25, 27, 33; application of, requires cooperation, 27; cooperation and threat of, 27; defined, 25; fear of, produces obedience, 28, 55; insufficient to maintain regime, 27; maintenance of political power and, 27; mutinies and, 70; noncooperation and willingness to suffer, 29; nonviolent, *see* nonviolent action/struggle; restricting ability to apply, 70. *See also* political jiujitsu, repression

Satyagraha, 48, 60. *See also* Gandhi; India

Severing, Carl, 15

Sit-ins, 46

Smrkovsky, Josef, 16

Social boycotts, 42, 89, 135. *See also* social noncooperation

Social defense. See civilian-based defense

Social distance, 60

Social noncooperation, 42, 92; "cold shoulder" practiced by Danes, 42; forms of, 42; in *Ruhrkampf*, 42

Social power: best guarantor of freedom, 33. *See also* civilian-based defense; nonviolent action/struggle

Sources of power, 23; authority, 24; denial of authority, 65; denial of skills and knowledge, 67–68; dependent on cooperation, 23; human resources, 24; intangible factors, 24; material resources, 24; removal of, 65–71; removal of human

About the Author _____

GENE SHARP, D.Phil. (Oxon.), is President of the Albert Einstein Institution, a nonprofit organization devoted to research, policy studies, and education about nonviolent struggle. He was previously Program Director, Program on Nonviolent Sanctions in Conflict and Defense, Center for International Affairs, Harvard University, and is Professor Emeritus of Political Science at Southeastern Massachusetts University.

He holds the degrees of Doctor of Philosophy in political theory from Oxford University, Master of Arts in Sociology from Ohio State University, and Bachelor of Arts in Social Sciences from Ohio State University. He lived for ten years in England and Norway before being invited to Harvard in 1965. He is an international lecturer and his writings have been translated into seventeen languages.